ALEXANDER ARNOLD

MATT AND TOM OLDFIELD

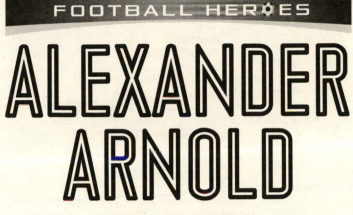

ULTIMATE
FOOTBALL HEROES

ALEXANDER ARNOLD

FROM THE PLAYGROUND
TO THE PITCH

DINO

First published by Dino Books in 2020,
an imprint of Bonnier Books UK,
The Plaza, 535 King's Road, London SW10 0SZ
Owned by Bonnier Books,
Sveavägen 56, Stockholm, Sweden

🐦 @dinobooks
🐦 @footieheroesbks
www.heroesfootball.com
www.bonnierbooks.co.uk

Text © Matt and Tom Oldfield 2020

The right of Matt and Tom Oldfield to be identified as the
authors of this work has been asserted by them in accordance
with the Copyright, Designs and Patents Act 1988.

Design by www.envydesign.co.uk

Paperback ISBN: 978 1 78946 240 1
E-book ISBN: 978 1 78946 241 8

British Library Cataloguing-in-Publication Data:
A catalogue record for this book is available from the British Library.

Printed and bound in Great Britain by Clays Ltd, Elcograf S.p.A.

3 5 7 9 10 8 6 4 2

For all readers, young and old(er)

ULTIMATE FOOTBALL HEROES

Matt Oldfield delivers sports writing workshops in schools, and is the author of *Unbelievable Football* and *Johnny Ball: Accidental Football Genius*. Tom Oldfield is a freelance sports writer and the author of biographies on Cristiano Ronaldo, Arsène Wenger and Rafael Nadal.

Cover illustration by Dan Leydon
To learn more about Dan visit danleydon.com
To purchase his artwork visit etsy.com/shop/footynews

TABLE OF CONTENTS

ACKNOWLEDGEMENTS

First of all, I'd like to thank Bonnier Books UK for supporting me supporting me throughout and for running the ever-expanding UFH ship so smoothly. Writing stories for the next generation of football fans is both an honour and a pleasure.

I wouldn't be doing this if it wasn't for my brother Tom. I owe him so much and I'm very grateful for his belief in me as an author. I feel like Robin setting out on a solo career after a great partnership with Batman. I hope I do him (Tom, not Batman) justice with these new books.

Next up, I want to thank my friends for keeping me sane during long hours in front of the laptop.

Pang, Will, Mills, Doug, John, Charlie – the laughs and the cups of coffee are always appreciated.

I've already thanked my brother but I'm also very grateful to the rest of my family, especially Melissa, Noah and of course Mum and Dad. To my parents, I owe my biggest passions: football and books. They're a real inspiration for everything I do.

Finally, I couldn't have done this without Iona's encouragement and understanding during long, work-filled weekends. Much love to you.

CHAPTER 1

THE MIRACLE OF ANFIELD

7 May 2019, Anfield, Liverpool

As Trent emerged from the team bus and walked towards the stadium entrance, he was greeted by a tremendous sight and sound. A red army had arrived early to welcome their Liverpool heroes to Anfield and to pass on an important message to the players:

'Come on, we can do this – we can beat Barcelona!'

Trent already believed his team could do it, and after that extraordinary show of support, how could they fail! Yes, Liverpool were 3–0 down after the

UEFA Champions League semi-final first leg against Lionel Messi and co, but so what? They were good enough to win 4–0, even without two of their star front three, Mohamed Salah and Roberto Firmino. At Anfield, anything was possible.

Liverpool! Liverpool! Liverpool!

As a local lad, Trent loved playing every home game, but European nights were extra special. The atmosphere, the anthem, the amazing opponents – that's what he had dreamed of, growing up in West Derby, and now it was a reality.

After watching from the bench in Barcelona, Trent couldn't wait to play his part this time. At six years old, in 2005, he had watched 'The Miracle of Istanbul' on TV at home with his family, when Liverpool faced AC Milan in that year's UEFA Champions League final. What an unforgettable night! He had cheered and cheered for his heroes – Steven Gerrard, Xabi Alonso, Jamie Carragher – as they fought back from 3–0 down to beat their Italian opponents on penalties.

Well now, it was time for another famous

Liverpool fightback. With the home crowd behind them, they were ready to give it everything to beat Barcelona and reach the Champions League Final once again.

'We *have* to win that trophy,' Trent thought to himself in the tunnel before kick-off. The memories of losing to Real Madrid in the 2018 final were still fresh and painful – Mo's injury, Gareth Bale's bicycle-kick and, of course, Loris Karius' errors. There was only one way to get rid of them: by returning to the biggest stage, and this time, becoming Champions of Europe.

As Liverpool's attacking right-back, Trent had a difficult, double challenge ahead of him. On the one hand, his manager, Jürgen Klopp, wanted him to push forward as much as possible, and deliver lots of his dangerous crosses. The Reds had to score four goals and he had already set up eleven in the Premier League, plus another two in the Champions League.

'Get the ball in the box whenever you can,' Sadio Mané told him. 'I'll be waiting!'

But first, Trent had to do his defensive work and

keep Messi, Luis Suárez, and Philippe Coutinho quiet. Because if Barcelona scored an away goal at Anfield, then it was game over for Liverpool. No, they couldn't let that happen.

'We've got to stay focused tonight!' Virgil van Dijk called out to his fellow defenders: Trent on the right, Andrew Robertson on the left, and in the middle, Joël Matip. One of the biggest games of their lives was about to begin.

With the sounds of 'You'll Never Walk Alone' still echoing around the stadium, Liverpool went straight on the attack. Sadio pounced on a Barcelona mistake and flicked it through to his captain, Jordan Henderson. Hendo's shot was saved, but Divock Origi scored the rebound. *3–1!*

What a start! Trent punched the air but there were no proper team celebrations. Instead, the Liverpool players ran straight back for the restart; they still had lots of work to do.

'That's it – keep going!' Klopp urged them on.

Thanks to some great goalkeeping from Alisson, the score was still 1–0 to Liverpool at half-time, but 3–1 to Barcelona on aggregate. Trent and his teammates now had forty-five minutes left to score at least two goals. Was it time for Klopp to change his tactics?

'Robbo, are you okay?' the manager called across the changing room.

The Liverpool left-back nodded but he was clearly hurt and hobbling. Klopp had to make a quick decision: 'Okay – Gini, you're coming on. Milly, I need you to move to left-back.'

As the second half started, Liverpool pushed forward on the attack again. So far, Trent had been solid at right-back, but not spectacular. What could he do to help his team to win? He tried to head the ball through to Divock, but it bounced to a Barcelona player instead.

'Rubbish!' Trent snarled at himself. He was so much better than that! But he didn't give up; not now, not ever. That's why Klopp trusted him, and why he was on track to reach his second Champions League Final before the age of twenty-one. But to get there, Liverpool still needed two more goals...

Trent used his determination to win the ball straight back and then dribbled forward up the right wing. What next? As he looked up to deliver the cross, he could only see Sadio in the middle, surrounded by three Barcelona players. No, Trent decided to wait a little longer, until there were more Liverpool shirts there too…

NOW! He crossed it just as Gini Wijnaldum burst into the box and *BANG!* he smashed the ball into the net first time. *3–2!* Game on!

It was like that match against AC Milan all over again – only this time, they also had the Anfield roar behind them. Suddenly, Barcelona were on the back foot and Liverpool looked unstoppable. Two minutes later, Xherdan Shaqiri crossed it from the left and their super sub Gini scored again. *3–3!*

Okay, now Liverpool could celebrate! Trent raced up the right wing to give Gini a great big hug. 'Yes, you hero – come onnnnnnn!'

What now? There were still almost forty minutes to go before extra time – should Liverpool sit deeper and defend for a bit, or go for the winner?

In the end, they went for a bit of both. Trent did chase back to help stop the Barcelona counterattacks, but he also continued to push forward whenever possible, knowing one more goal would win it. When he couldn't find a way past Sergi Roberto on the wing, Trent cleverly booted the ball against him instead. *Corner-kick!*

As he placed the ball down on the spot, he thought about taking it himself. After all, Trent's incredible corners had been causing problems for the Barcelona defence all game. But that was from the other side of the pitch; wouldn't it be better for Xherdan to curl this one in with his left foot instead?

Just as Trent began to walk away from the ball, he spotted something. In the box, the Barcelona players had all switched off. What if he could catch them by surprise? Trent was always looking for ways to outsmart his opponents and here was a perfect opportunity. Divock was free and standing in a great position to score. There was nothing to lose for Liverpool and everything to gain!

Trent didn't even give Divock a shout; there

wasn't time for that. No, he just spun around and crossed the ball in quickly, hoping for the best. Luckily, Divock was alert and he guided the ball into the top corner before the Barcelona defenders could close him down. 4–3!

Liverpool had done it – what a phenomenal fightback! Up in the Anfield stands, the club's supporters went wild and so did the players on the pitch. They rushed over to form a big, team huddle around their two match-winning heroes. What a finish from Divock and what quick-thinking from Trent! For a twenty-year-old to try something like that in a Champions League semi-final was astonishing.

'You're a genius!' Gini cried out.

Barcelona had lost their focus and let Liverpool back into the game. Now, Trent and his fellow defenders had to avoid making the same mistake. If they could just hold on for another fifteen minutes, they would be through to their second Champions League Final in a row. With the home crowd urging them on, they stayed strong until at last the final whistle blew.

'Yeeeeeesss!' Trent let out a long loud roar into the Liverpool sky and then ran over to celebrate with his teammates. They had done it; he had done it – his two smart assists had saved the day.

'CHAMPIONS LEAGUE FINAL, HERE WE COME!' they all cheered together.

Fourteen years on from 'The Miracle of Istanbul', Liverpool now had a new one to add to their collection: 'The Miracle of Anfield'. From 3–0 down, they had fought back brilliantly to beat Messi's Barcelona 4–3. Unbelievable!

It was a night that none of those proud players would ever, ever forget. Least of all Trent, the lad from Liverpool, a life-long Red and now a local hero.

CHAPTER 2

THE MOST COMPETITIVE KIDS IN LIVERPOOL

'Go on, try and tackle me, Trent – I bet you can't!'

'Yes, I can, Tyler!'

From the kitchen, Dianne could hear every kick and cry, the happy – and not-so happy – sounds of her young sons playing their favourite game: football.

'Boys – play nice!'

She knew that letting them play indoor football would probably end in disputes and disaster, but on rainy days like this one, it was the only option. Even the front garden was a no-go zone, and her husband, Michael, was away working in London, so he couldn't take the boys across the road to play in the park.

Indoor football it was then. This way, Tyler and Trent could use up some of their endless energy, while Dianne kept an eye – or at least an ear – on them. Plus, how much damage could two boys do with a soft, spongy ball...

CRASH!

'Sorry, Mam!' Dianne heard Tyler call out.

'What was that?' she asked, rushing into the living room.

Luckily, it was only an old lamp that no-one really liked anyway; she had already removed any items that she really cared about. She knew what her sons were like when it came to football. Crazy!

At the dinner table or in the classroom, Tyler and Trent were nice, normal, polite young children, but that all changed when they played football, and especially when they played football *together*, 1 vs 1. Suddenly, they became the most competitive kids in the whole of Liverpool. They would do anything to win:

Slide tackles that gave them carpet burns,

Shirt pulls that left holes in their favourite football

kits, and shoves that led to broken lamps and bruised little bodies.

'It wasn't me,' Trent whined, looking up at his mum with his innocent face on. 'It was him – he pushed me!'

Tyler was four years older, and so four years stronger, despite Trent's dogged determination.

Dianne sighed loudly: 'Right, that's your last warning, boys, okay? If I hear one more foul or fall-out, then I'm taking the ball away.'

It was a threat that she had used before and it always worked. Noooooooooo – for Tyler and Trent, no more football was the worst thing imaginable!

'Please Mam, I promise we'll be good!'

'Yes, I promise too!'

The peace would last for about ten minutes, until passing back and forth got boring, and then the boys would go back to being crazily competitive again.

'FIRST TO FIVE GOALS WINS – GO!'

The brotherly battles got even fiercer when their brother, Marcel, was born. Now they could play 2 vs 1s, or even Wembley singles, and Dianne and

Michael had triple football trouble to deal with!

On rainy days, the Alexander-Arnold family home was like a mix between an obstacle course and a haunted house. Dianne never knew when one of her boys would burst around the corner, dribbling some kind of ball at their feet – tennis, tinfoil, even rolled-up socks.

'Watch out, Mam – I'm winning!'

And if one brother appeared, then there would always be at least one more chasing behind them.

'Woah, sorry, Mam – I've got to stop Trent from scoring!'

As much as Dianne loved her lively sons, she did long for a bit of peace and quiet every now and again. So, one rainy day when they were all stuck indoors, she asked Michael to teach the boys how to play chess. At least that was a calmer, sit-down game for them to get crazily competitive about.

And as their dad explained to them in their very first lesson, chess wasn't so different from football really. 'In fact, the key ideas are the same,' Michael told them. 'You've got to stay calm and clever under pressure and stick to your strategy if you want to win.'

Cool! That got the boys' attention. They listened carefully and learned the rules quickly. In no time at all, their sibling chess battles had begun.

'Yes, I beat you – in your face, bro!' Trent shouted, almost tipping over the board in his excitement.

It didn't matter what he was doing, he just loved that winning feeling. And so did Tyler, which is why, when he lost to Trent, he stormed straight off to his bedroom to sulk.

'Did you see that, Dad?' Trent beamed with pride. 'I destroyed him with my mind!'

Michael smiled. 'Well done, son – maybe one day you'll be the next Garry Kasparov!'

Trent frowned. 'Who?'

'He's a famous chess grandmaster, probably the greatest player of all time.'

Trent shook his head. He liked chess, but he LOVED football. 'No thanks Dad, I want to be the next Steven Gerrard!'

CHAPTER 3

MELWOOD MOTIVATION

Steven Gerrard was a local legend and Trent's favourite footballer by far. He even had a Liverpool shirt with '8 GERRARD' on the back, and posters of him all over his bedroom wall. Gerrard was a box-to-box midfielder who played the game with so much energy, passion, and skill. He could do it all: pass, tackle, dribble, *and* shoot.

'Just like me!'

Trent and his brothers recreated Gerrard's greatest goals over and over again in the park, taking it in turns to play the leading role. The luckiest one would get to be the star himself, the second luckiest would pretend to be whichever teammate had provided the assist, and the third and final brother would get the less exciting job of being the commentator:

'Liverpool are leading 2–1 here at Anfield, with ten minutes to go,' Tyler began, using his hand as an imaginary microphone. As the oldest, he was the best at the speaking bit. Plus, he knew that Marcel would get upset and cry if he didn't get to play one of the main parts.

'But 2–1 isn't good enough, from Liverpool's point of view. They'll need to score a third to make it through to the Champions League Last 16...'

That was Tyler's cue to kick off the action. He had two roles to play in this particular scene: commentator, and Jamie Carragher – another local Liverpool legend.

'Here's Carragher, just trying to stay cool,' Tyler said, while dribbling the ball down the left wing past imaginary opponents. Then, with a look up, he curled a cross towards 'Neil Mellor', otherwise known as Marcel who was too young to really know what was going on, but loved joining in with his brothers' games. Plus, his instructions were simple:

'Pass it to Trent!'

'Mellor!' Tyler's commentary continued. 'Lovely cushioned header...'

Marcel didn't like heading yet, so he kicked the ball instead. That didn't matter, just as long as it travelled in the right direction.

'...for GERRRAAAAAARRD!'

Trent had practised this part many times to make it pretty much perfect. He took a short run-up towards the ball, focused on the target, and then BANG! he struck his shot low and hard, just like Stevie G. It flew through the air and into the bottom right corner. Every time.

'YA BEAUUUTYYYYY,' Tyler continued, putting on a different voice to play the other commentator. 'WHAT A HIT, SON!'

GOOOOOOAAAAALLLLLL!!!!!!!! Their dad was away, so there was no goalkeeper, but Trent was sure that no-one could have saved it anyway. It was unstoppable! Now, for the next part: the celebration. He raced away towards the imaginary fans, with his arms up and out like a hero. When he reached the edge of the field, he added in an extra bit from another of Gerrard's great goals: a knee slide.

What a feeling! Even pretending to be Stevie G was loads of fun, so what would it be like to actually be him? There was only one way to find out. Trent was desperate to see his hero up close and he had a plan to make that happen.

The Alexander-Arnolds lived in a part of Liverpool called West Derby. It was quite a long way away from Anfield, the club's stadium, but the team's training ground, Melwood, was only just around the corner! In fact, if the boys peeked through the fence, or even better, stood on top of the bins in the garden, they could catch a glimpse of the players practising.

'Woah, look that's Xabi Alonso!'

'And there's Djibril Cissé!'

'AND THERE'S STEVIE G!'

Trent and his brothers spent hours watching the training sessions, or 'spying' as their mum liked to call it. Sometimes, there wasn't much for them to see, but it was still worth it, even for a quick sighting. It was so cool and exciting to be so close to their football heroes every day!

And inspiring too. For Trent, their Melwood spying acted as an extra motivation to achieve his dreams. Not that he really needed it, though. Even at the age of six, he was already totally serious about playing professional football for his local club.

'That's going to be me one day!' he told his brothers, pointing at the Liverpool players in the distance.

'And me!'

'And me!'

Trent smiled and looked down at the Liverpool shirt he was wearing. 'Right, well we've got work to do then! Come on, let's go and practise in the park. I'll be Stevie G.'

Tyler groaned. 'Bro, you're always Stevie G – it's not fair!'

CHAPTER 4

LIVERPOOL'S LUCKY BOY

Young Trent had decided on his dream, but how was he actually going to achieve it? Hmm, he hadn't worked that part out yet. Maybe he could just knock on the door at Melwood and ask for a game with Gerrard...

Luckily, before he tried that approach, a much better opportunity came along.

Trent's school, St Matthew's Primary, sat roughly halfway between Anfield and Melwood, and had strong connections with Liverpool Football Club. They were running a coaching camp during the school holidays at the club's academy and invited some of the St Matthew's pupils to come along.

When their headteacher stood up in the assembly hall and asked who would like to attend, almost every hand shot up in the air straight away. What a silly question! They all loved football, and Liverpool in particular. During their playground matches, a few defenders would pretend to be Carragher, a few strikers (or goal hangers) would pretend to be Michael Owen, and the rest? Stevie G, of course! But whatever their position, they all wanted to play for the greatest football club in the world...

LIVERPOOL! LIVERPOOL!

Usually, the children were on their best behaviour during assembly time, but one mention of the 'L' word had sent them wild with excitement. Who knew, maybe they'd even get to meet the famous players?

'Pick me! Pick me!' Trent muttered to himself as he strained to keep his arm up for as long as possible. It was a competition and so he was desperate to win.

Eventually, the headteacher called for calm and quiet. 'Okay, well seeing as there's so much interest, I think the fairest thing would be to pick names out of a hat.'

Noooooo! Surely, they should just pick the school's best young footballers? That way, Trent would definitely make the list, even though he was still only six. But no, instead he would just have to hope…

As the lucky names were read out, Trent sat there with his eyes closed and his fingers firmly crossed. 'Please pick me! Pleeeeaaaase!'

'…Paul McManus…'

'…Megan Wilson…'

'…Michael Doyle…'

Then, just when he was starting to lose hope…

'…and finally… Trent Alexander-Arnold.'

'Yes!' he cheered, punching the air with joy. What an amazing opportunity – he was going to train with Liverpool!

When the big day arrived, Dianne dropped Trent off at the academy and wished him luck. Luck? No, it was luck that had got him this chance in the first place; now it was all about talent. He was ready to prove to the academy coaches what a promising young player he was. 'The next Stevie G!' he thought to himself.

Trent felt a little nervous when he first arrived and saw so many unfamiliar faces around him, but as soon as the training session began, he was fully focused on football. As possibly the most competitive kid in Liverpool, he was determined to be the best at every single drill: running, passing, tackling, dribbling, and shooting. If he didn't ace the activity first time, then he made sure that he did the second time.

'Right, let's play some five-a-side matches!' the coaches announced at last.

This was the part that Trent has been waiting for. He raced around the pitch like he was still in his living room at home, batting for every ball like he was playing against his brothers. His energy was endless and so was his determination. Nothing and no-one were going to stop him from winning the tournament and becoming a Liverpool legend.

GOAL!

'Well played, son!'

It didn't take long for the coaches to spot Trent's talent. Although the main aim of the camp was to give something back to the local community, the club was always on the lookout for stand-out young players. Kids who could control the ball well, pass and move, and play the game with confidence.

'Wow, who's that?' asked Ian Barrigan. He was Liverpool's 'Head of pre-Academy Recruitment', which meant that he was in charge of spotting the brightest young kids, the ones who really stood out above the rest. He was pointing at a boy who looked very promising indeed. With his athleticism and technique, he was far too good for this level.

The coach looked down at the list of names on his clipboard. 'That's Trent Alexander-Arnold.'

When Dianne came back to collect her son at the end of the first day of camp, Barrigan was there waiting to speak to her.

'Trent has been terrific today,' he said with a big smile. 'A star in the making, we reckon! We'd like him to come and train with our Under-7s every week, if that's okay with you?'

Dianne looked down at her son's wide, excited eyes and laughed. 'I think that's a yes – he'd love to. Thank you very much!'

It had all started with a bit of luck at school, and now, a few weeks later, Trent's Liverpool career was about to kick off.

CHAPTER 5

FIRST ANFIELD ADVENTURE

Now that Trent was 'a Liverpool player', as he proudly told everyone he met, he thought more and more about Anfield. 'Anfield' – the local people whispered it like it was a magic word and they spoke about it like it was a magical place. Was it really, though? From the outside, it looked like any other stadium to him: huge and concrete. But there had to be more to it than that.

Whenever the family drove past, he stared out of the car window up at the iconic building, wondering, 'What's it like inside?' In April 2005, Trent finally found out the answer – and yes, it really was a magical place!

It was the best surprise ever, the greatest gift they had ever received. Somehow, Dianne had managed to get Tyler and Trent tickets to watch Liverpool play in the Champions League quarter-final against Italian giants, Juventus! When they found out, they danced around the house for hours.

'Thanks Mam, you're the best!' they cheered, giving her the biggest hugs ever.

'Enjoy it, boys, but make sure you behave yourselves, okay?'

'Yes Mam, we will!'

Time seemed to tick by so slowly as they waited for their Anfield adventure to begin. But at last, they were on their way, wearing their red Liverpool shirts underneath their coats. During the journey, they talked excitedly about who would play (Igor Bišćan or Xabi Alonso? Vladimir Šmicer or Anthony Le Tallec?) and who would win (Liverpool, of course, but by how many goals?).

'2–0, I reckon.'

'Nah, 3–1!'

But no sooner had the boys entered the stadium,

their chatter stopped completely, and they fell silent
as they looked out at the wondrous sights. Anfield
was amazing! Even though all around them the stands
were still filling up, they had never seen so many
people in one place. And down below, they could see
the Liverpool players warming up on the biggest, most
beautiful football pitch they had ever seen. Spying at
Melwood was nothing compared to this!

Trent tried his best to take everything in so that he
would remember it the next day to tell all his friends,
but the whole experience seemed so unreal. He
turned to Tyler with a massive smile on his face. They
didn't say a word to each other; they didn't need to.

If the sights of Anfield were awesome, the sounds
were even better. As kick-off approached, the singing
and chanting got louder and louder, until it felt like
the stadium was actually moving! The energy coming
from the Kop End was extraordinary.

Then came the most powerful moment of all: 'You'll
Never Walk Alone'. As the 40,000 Liverpool fans sang
the famous club song together, Trent could feel the
hairs on the back of his neck standing up. Wow! In

his head, he tried to imagine what it would be like to walk out on to the pitch as a Liverpool player, listening to such inspiring sounds from the fans.

'I would be so fired up,' Trent told himself, 'that I would win every game!'

It wasn't quite that easy, though, especially against a top team like Juventus, who had world-class players in every position: Gianluigi Buffon in goal, Fabio Cannavaro in defence, Pavel Nedvěd in midfield, and Alessandro Del Piero and Zlatan Ibrahimović in attack. Wow, The Reds were really going to need the home crowd cheering them on.

LIVERPOOL! LIVERPOOL! LIVERPOOL!

Tyler and Trent clapped and cheered along with everyone else. And ten minutes into the match, things got even better. Luis García flicked on Stevie G's corner and there was Sami Hyypiä at the back post to volley the ball in. 1–0!

'Hurraaaaaaaay!'

Trent had never heard a roar like it. It was deafening! He turned to say something to Tyler, but the words were lost in the Anfield atmosphere. All around them, people were hugging and dancing and singing, so they climbed up on their seats to get a better view of the celebrations below.

LIVERPOOL! LIVERPOOL! LIVERPOOL!

Tyler and Trent felt on top of the world.

Fifteen minutes later, García scored a screamer to make it 2–0 to Liverpool. 'WHAT A GOAL!' the brothers shouted at each other as Anfield erupted again. Their eyes were wide with excitement; they couldn't believe what they were watching.

Sadly, that was the last of the Liverpool goals that night. In the second half, Juventus fought back and so they had lots of nerve-wracking defending to do, especially when Cannavaro scored to make it 2–1. For the last five minutes, Trent could hardly bear to watch. What if Juventus got another goal? He would be devastated!

But no, Liverpool stayed strong to win the first leg. 'Get in!' Tyler and Trent cheered together at the final whistle, feeling tired and emotional.

What a magical night – the first of many, hopefully! When they got home, Trent hardly slept a wink because his brain was too busy replaying every moment of the match and showing him his own football future.

Walking out in the famous red shirt, with the Anfield roar in his ears, and then scoring the winning goal. Yes, that's what Trent wanted to do when he was older.

CHAPTER 6

MAY 2005: THE TROPHY AND THE BUS TOUR

Following Trent's amazing first Anfield adventure, Liverpool's Champions League journey continued. First, the team travelled to Italy for the quarter-final second leg against Juventus, where they defended heroically to earn a 0–0 draw, even without the injured Stevie G. That was enough to take them through to the semi-finals.

'LIVERPOOL! LIVERPOOL! LIVERPOOL!' the Alexander-Arnold brothers chanted as they danced around the living room at full-time. They were now bigger fans than ever.

Next up: their English rivals, Chelsea. They had John Terry, Frank Lampard, and Didier Drogba, plus they were top of the Premier League table, but Trent was still full of belief. Liverpool had Carragher, Xabi Alonso, and Stevie G, plus the best supporters in the world.

'We can beat anyone!' he declared confidently ahead of kick-off.

However, the first leg at Stamford Bridge was so tight and tense that Trent could hardly watch the TV screen. What if Chelsea scored? Drogba and Lampard both had great chances, but neither could get past Liverpool's brilliant backline.

'Sami, you legend!' Trent cheered as Hyypiä made another superb saving tackle. Up until then, he had always dreamed of becoming a box-to-box midfielder like Stevie G, but maybe being a defender wouldn't be so bad...

The first leg finished 0–0; now, Liverpool just had to win back home at Anfield. 'Easy!' Trent thought to himself. And with the loud crowd cheering them on, the Reds made a strong start to the match. John Arne Riise passed it infield to Stevie G, who chipped a beautiful ball through to Milan Baroš.

'Yes, yes, go on!' the Alexander-Arnolds shouted at the screen.

The Liverpool striker managed to lift it over the Chelsea keeper, but the ball bounced down in the six-yard box. Who would react the quickest? Luis García! The Spaniard raced in and fired a shot, which deflected off Terry and flew towards the goal line…

'It's in! It's in!' Trent cried, jumping off the sofa in excitement.

William Gallas got back to clear the ball away, but had it already crossed the line? Yes, the referee had given the goal – *1–0!*

Hurraaaaaaaay!

As the Liverpool players celebrated on the pitch at Anfield, the Alexander-Arnolds celebrated in their living room in West Derby, with the same levels of passion.

'Yes, we're going to play in the Champions League final!' Marcel screamed.

First, however, their team had eighty-six more minutes of football to get through. Chelsea attacked and attacked, but once again, they couldn't find a way past Liverpool's brilliant backline. At last, the final whistle blew. The club's players and supporters could breathe a huge sigh of relief and then look forward to a big night in Istanbul.

'We did it! We're in the Champions League Final!'

Trent couldn't wait to watch it. His heroes had done so well to get this far, but now, to win the trophy, they would have to beat the best team in the world, AC Milan. Although Trent was still too young to know the names of all the top international footballers, even he had heard of:

Cafú,

Paolo Maldini,

Kaká,

Hernán Crespo,

Andriy Shevchenko.

And who did they all play for? AC Milan. Wow, what a line-up! It was going to be a very tough test for Liverpool's brilliant backline. Could they stay strong, just like they had against Juventus and Chelsea?

No, by half-time, Liverpool were losing 3–0 and Trent and his brothers looked heartbroken.

How could football be so cruel? They thought about switching off the TV and going to bed, but fortunately, they didn't. They were still there, watching on the sofa, as Liverpool launched their incredible comeback.

First, Gerrard scored a powerful, leaping header. *3–1!*

'Yes, Stevie G!' Trent cheered, punching the air. At least his team had got one goal.

But then two minutes later, Vladimír Šmicer went for a dipping long-range shot and the ball squirmed under Dida's arms and into the bottom corner. *3–2!*

Trent's eyes lit up with hope again. Woah, Liverpool couldn't… could they? But there was no time for thinking; the Reds were already on the attack again. Stevie G raced into the box to reach Baroš' clever backheel, but just as he was about to shoot, an AC Milan player fouled him.

'PENALTY!' the Alexander-Arnolds all yelled together. Yes, the referee pointed to the spot. Dida dived down low to save Xabi Alonso's penalty, but the Spaniard slid in to score the rebound. It was 3–3 – Liverpool's comeback was complete!

'Yes, we're going to win this! We're going to win this!' Trent and his brothers roared as they jumped up and down, way too excited to sit still.

Michael looked over at his celebrating sons and smiled. 'Enjoy this moment, because you lucky boys are watching one of the best football matches EVER!'

It was a night that none of them would ever forget, and it wasn't over yet. Liverpool's backline had to be at their brilliant best to stop AC Milan attack after AC Milan attack.

'Keep going, Carra!'

'Well done, Dudek!'

Somehow, the scoreline stayed at 3–3 until the final whistle, and then all the way through extra time too. The 2005 Champions League Final was going to penalties!

Michael wasn't sure that his sons could handle any more heartbreak. Surely, after that incredible comeback, Liverpool had to win it?

And luckily, they did. Shevchenko stepped up to take AC Milan's crucial spot-kick …and Dudek dived down low to make a super save! At last, it was all over; Liverpool were the new Champions of Europe!

'Come onnnnnnn!'

Trent and his brothers were allowed to stay up way past their bedtime to watch their team's trophy celebrations. They didn't want to miss a thing and besides, they were far too excited for sleep anyway.

'Campeones, Campeones, Olé! Olé! Olé!'

First, the Melwood motivation, then the Anfield adventure, and now this – Istanbul inspiration! Trent's mind was made up. Whatever it took, he was going to grow up to become a Liverpool star. He didn't just want to play for his local club; no, he wanted to win lots and lots of trophies with them.

'Imagine how good it would feel to lift the CHAMPIONS LEAGUE!' he said to Tyler as they sat on the front step of their house the next day, wearing *their Liverpool shirts, an*d waiting for the bus to arrive.

They had been waiting ages already but that didn't matter. It would be worth it because this wasn't just any old bus; it was the Liverpool team bus, carrying their football heroes on a tour of the city to show off their shiny new trophy. And it was going to come right past their road! They would happily wait all week in order to see that.

But suddenly, their trophy-winning daydreams were interrupted by a shout from further down the street: 'IT'S COMING!'

In a flash, Trent was up on his feet and watching out for the first sign of red. Yes, there it was! As the bus slowly made its way towards them, the cheers grew louder and louder and so did the beating of Trent's heart. Carra, Xabi Alonso, Stevie G – there were all his Liverpool heroes, holding the Champions League trophy, and they were almost close enough for him to touch. What an unbelievable buzz!

'One day,' Trent told himself once that thrilling moment was over, 'I want to be on the top deck of one of those buses.'

CHAPTER 7

FOOTBALL, FOOTBALL, FOOTBALL

Fired up by the trophy and the bus tour, Trent was a boy on a serious, sporting mission – to become 'the next Stevie G', Liverpool's next local superstar. And how was he going to achieve his goal? By playing as much football as possible.

During the week, Trent trained with Liverpool, but he was still too young to sign a contract with the club, so at the weekends, they let him play for other teams too. Three other teams actually, including one of the top local clubs, Country Park.

'Are you sure you want to play another match today?' his parents and coaches would ask, but his energy was endless, especially when there were goals to score and games to win.

'Yes, I do!'

Not only was Trent spending hours and hours on the football field each weekend, but he was also playing in the most tiring position. With his speed, skill and determination, he was the perfect fit for the box-to-box midfield role, just like his hero Stevie G. So, one minute, he was racing forward to set up goals for the strikers, and the next, he was chasing back to stop goals at the other end. He wanted to be involved in everything, and why not? He could do it all and he wasn't even seven years old yet!

'Hey, take it easy, son,' the Country Park coach often had to tell him once they were winning comfortably. 'Give these guys a chance – go play at centre-back for a bit!'

Although Trent was a quiet, modest kid, both on and off the pitch, his football talent was already clear for all to see. That's why Liverpool signed him up as soon as they could, to stop the Everton and Manchester United scouts from stealing him away.

Not that Trent would have thought about joining

any other club; he was Liverpool for life! But it was still a fantastic feeling to make that official.

'Something tells me you'll be here for a long time!' Barrigan said with a smile.

'I hope so!' Trent replied eagerly.

In most ways, he was a coach's dream. He was the first one on the training field and the last one off it: a fast learner who worked hard and always wanted to improve. There was only one thing that got him into trouble: he was a terrible loser.

Trent treated every single football match like it was his last ever brotherly battle. He was still Liverpool's most competitive kid, and on the few occasions when he didn't win, he really lost his cool.

'Come on, Trent, it's just a game!' the coaches would try to tell him as he stormed off the field, but for him, there was no such thing. A defeat was a failure; it was as simple as that. When he lost, he was an absolute nightmare to be around – no words, no food, only scowls and stomps. His bad moods often lasted for days, and sometimes Dianne would have to use her most dangerous threat of all – no football.

'Sorry, Trent won't be able to play this week,' she'd tell Barrigan on the phone. 'He's not been behaving well at all.'

That was usually enough to get her son eating and talking again.

The Liverpool coaches weren't too worried about Trent's moods when it came to losing. They figured it was something he'd grow out of eventually. And besides, being super-competitive wasn't a bad thing. He just had to learn to channel it in the right way. So, in training, if Trent's team was winning easily, Barrigan started giving a few penalties to their opponents to even up the score. At first, Trent reacted angrily every time:

'No way, that's a joke. I'm not playing anymore!'

But eventually, he learned to see it as a challenge instead. If his coach was going to cheat, then he would just have to raise his game and find a way to win anyway. Usually, that worked a treat.

'Well done, lad. See, you didn't lose your cool that time. Instead, you used your competitive spirit to spur you on – much better!'

Trent was improving every single aspect of his game. He really was a Liverpool superstar in the making. As he got older, the club asked him to cut down on the number of matches he played for his other teams, but that didn't mean he was lazing around on the sofa. No, his life was still football, football, football. If he wasn't out on the pitch, winning with Country Park, then he was probably out in the garden, battling with his brothers.

'FIRST TO TEN GOALS WINS – GO!'

The only thing that would stop the Alexander-Arnold boys playing was a really bad injury, or the ball flying over the fence for the thousandth time.

'Sorry!' all three would shout out, and then the heated arguments would begin.

'Not again! Quick, go round and get it, bro.'

'Me? Why me? You kicked it over!'

'Come on, just do it! Or won't Liverpool let you?'

'Shut up – you do it!'

'No, you!'

'BOYS!'

As annoying as his brothers could be sometimes,

they would always be Trent's favourite people to play with, or against. It was definitely better than kicking a ball against a wall on his own! Where would he be without them? Probably not on his way to becoming a Liverpool superstar, that's for sure.

CHAPTER 8

FROM ATTACK TO DEFENCE TO MIDFIELD

The Liverpool coaches all agreed that Trent had a bright football future ahead of him. There was no question about that; he was one of the club's most promising young players. Already, at the age of twelve, he was showing the talent, athleticism, and dedication it would have taken for him to become a top professional when he was older. However, what they couldn't agree on was his best position on the pitch.

Central midfielder? That's where Trent played for Country Park in the local Sunday league. He loved the Stevie G role, running box-to-box all game long.

Striker? That's where he usually played for his

secondary school, St Mary's, scoring goal after goal with his fierce right foot.

Right winger? That's where he normally played for the Liverpool Under-12s because he was really fast, and he could cross the ball into the box so well. But was that really where he belonged?

The problem was that Trent was such a gifted and hard-working footballer that he could play anywhere and still put in a top performance! It was certainly a nice problem for the Liverpool academy to have.

Trent himself hadn't yet decided what position he wanted to play. He was happy to play anywhere, to be honest, just as long as he was out on the pitch, proudly wearing the Liverpool shirt and winning every week. Well, actually, maybe not as goalkeeper...

When Trent moved up to the Under-14s, the coach tried him at centre-back instead. It was a big change from right wing, but he was a fast learner and he proved once again that he could play in any position they asked him to. He wasn't the tallest or the strongest, but he read the game really well for such a young player and there was no-one braver in the tackle. *CRUNCH!*

'Great challenge, Trent!'

So, was he all set to become 'The Next Jamie Carragher'? No, after two years with the Under-14s, Trent moved up to the Under-16s, where his new coach, Pep Lijnders, decided to play him in another new position: defensive midfield, the Number 6 at the base of the diamond. Less Stevie G, more Xabi Alonso.

'Cool, I love Alonso!'

In his new role, Trent could combine his brilliant football brain and perfect passing to control the game for Liverpool, while also using his endless energy to get forward to create chances for his teammates. It turned out to be his favourite position so far, especially as Lijnders also gave him the captain's armband to wear.

'Thanks, Coach!'

What an honour! Liverpool captain – tick! It was already another dream come true for Trent early in his football career. He wasn't getting carried away, though. He knew that he still had lots of hard work ahead of him.

But the Liverpool first team didn't feel so far away now. The more games Trent played in his new position, the better he became and the more he built up his confidence on the ball. Soon, he really felt at home at the heart of the midfield. Pass and move, pass and move – yes, he could definitely become 'The Next Xabi Alonso'! He was still learning all the time, and luckily Trent had Lijnders there to help him improve. The two of them got on really well, right from the start. The young Norwegian coach shared his serious, non-stop passion for football.

'Fancy a kickaround, Pep?' Trent often asked at the end of a tiring training session, as the other players headed home.

'Sure!'

On most days, they were the last to leave the academy training ground. For Trent, it was just like playing with his brothers, but a bit less competitive. Only a tiny bit, though! One on ones, head tennis, free kicks, two-touch passing – they practised them all for hours. Sometimes, they were having so much football fun together that they totally lost track of time and were still there when the floodlights were turned off.

'Same again tomorrow, Pep?'

'Sure!'

There was just no end to Trent's football energy and enthusiasm. He always wanted to be playing and improving, making progress towards that Liverpool first team.

Although football was a priority, Trent never let his schoolwork slip. His parents made sure of that. Their son needed good grades, as well as good skills. So, if he missed a class to go and train with Liverpool, then he had to catch up later: during breaktimes, lunchtimes, or after school, while his friends were out playing football without him.

It was hard sometimes, but Trent only had to picture himself walking out at Anfield as a Liverpool player to know that the sacrifices would be worth it in the end!

CHAPTER 9

COMPLIMENTS FROM A LIVERPOOL LEGEND

A nervous hush fell over the Liverpool Under-16s squad one evening when a very famous face appeared at practice… STEVIE G! Woah, what was he doing there?

'Right guys, you all know who this Liverpool legend is, so I won't bother introducing him,' Lijnders laughed as he looked out at all the awestruck faces. 'Stevie is doing his coaching qualifications at the moment, so he'll be helping out with our training sessions for the next few weeks. You lucky lads – make the most of having him here!'

Trent was still a quiet kid on a usual day, so on this extra-special day, he was star-struck into total silence. And so were all his teammates. Stevie G at *their*

training session – was this really happening? Surely, it was too good to be true. But no, there he was, only a few metres away. Trent thought back to his younger years, and all those hours he'd spent pretending to be Gerrard in the park and then spying on him practising at Melwood. And now look – they were standing on the same pitch. Unbelievable!

'Wait until I tell Tyler and Marcel about this!' he thought to himself.

Trent was too shy to speak to his hero, so instead he let his football skills do the talking. He tried to keep things simple during all of the training drills. Pass and move, pass and move, then run, tackle, run!

But it wasn't easy acting normal when the one and only Stevie G was there on the sidelines, clapping and cheering, 'Nice work!'

'Wow, is he saying that to *ME*?' Trent wondered. As the training session went on, his fears about making mistakes were replaced by an eagerness to impress. That super-competitive spirit kicked in as he raced around the field with a spring in his step, battling for every ball and showing off his full range of perfect passes. What an amazing opportunity this was – after all, he didn't get to play in front of a Liverpool legend every day!

'Make the most of having him here,' Trent muttered under his breath, repeating his coach's earlier advice. That's exactly what he was going to do.

After setting up a goal for his team with a beautiful through-ball, Trent looked over to see Lijnders and Gerrard deep in conversation. What were they talking about, or more importantly, who were they talking about? Him hopefully! Not only was he a midfielder and the team captain, but he was also a local lad. Yes, him and Stevie had so much in common. If he could stand out above the other academy players, then maybe Gerrard would even tell Liverpool's first-team manager, Brendan Rodgers, about him...

'No, don't get ahead of yourself now!' Trent told himself off. It was so far so good for 'Project Impress Stevie G', but one awesome assist wasn't enough. He had to keep shining until the very end.

And into extra time too. As well as a great chance to impress, the training session also turned out to be a great chance for him to learn. Because Stevie G stayed behind afterwards to do some long-range passing with the young players. *PING! PING! PING!* No matter the distance, no matter the angle, he was always deadly accurate, and he made it look so easy. Up close, it was incredible to see – how did he get it right every time?

'Practice,' was his answer. 'Hours and hours of practice.' Trent smiled and looked over at Pep – yes, they could definitely do that! He was already pretty good at switching the play from side to side, but practice would make those long passes perfect.

Trent listened carefully to Gerrard's every word and looked closely at every aspect of his technique. He wanted to remember every little movement, so that he could recreate it later.

Although Stevie G was only with them for a few training sessions, that was enough for Trent to achieve his aim. He had successfully impressed a Liverpool legend. It wasn't just his talent and athleticism; it was also his hunger for the game, and his fearlessness on the pitch. The kid clearly wasn't afraid of anything.

When Stevie published his new book a year later, he wrote about the future of his football club, and he picked out one young player in particular:

'Trent Arnold has a terrific chance of making it as a top professional.'

CHAPTER 10

EARLY INTERNATIONAL ADVENTURES WITH ENGLAND

Steven Gerrard wasn't the only one impressed by Trent's tremendous talent. So was John Peacock, the Head Coach of the England Under-17s. In April 2015, he announced his squad to compete in the upcoming European Championships:

From Arsenal, Chris Willock and Stephy Mavididi,

From Chelsea, Jay Dasilva and Ike Ugbo,

From Everton, James Yates, Nathan Holland, and Tom Davies…

…and from Liverpool, Herbie Kane and… Trent Alexander-Arnold!

'Get in!' Trent cheered proudly when he heard the news. It was such an honour to wear the Three Lions on his shirt and represent his country. It wasn't Trent's first England call-up – he had already played six times for the Under-16s – but it would be his first big Euro competition, his first international adventure away from home. The first of many, hopefully, because if England could make it through to the Euro semi-finals, they'd qualify for October's Under-17 World Cup in Chile.

'No problem, let's do this!' Trent told Herbie confidently as the squad set off for Bulgaria.

However, it wasn't quite as easy as he was expecting. There was one problem that Trent had to tackle straight away – working his way into the starting line-up. Unlike Liverpool, England often only played with two central midfielders and there were five of them fighting for those spots: Tayo Edun and Daniel Wright, as well as Tom Davies, Herbie, and Trent.

'Don't worry, you'll all get a chance to play,' their coach promised them.

For their opening 1–0 win over Italy, Peacock picked Tom and Herbie to start, only bringing Trent off the bench for the final five minutes. It was hardly long enough for him to even touch the ball, but in their second match against the Netherlands, he got to play from the start. This time, Peacock played a three-man midfield against Reda Boultam, Carel Eiting and Dani de Wit, who were all from the famous Ajax academy.

'Let the battle begin!' Trent cheered before kick-off.

It all started so well. England were winning 1–0, until early in the second half, when Trent rushed across to tackle de Wit, who had dribbled his way into the penalty area. At the last second, he slipped, and fell towards the Dutchman, who threw himself to the floor. Penalty!

'No way, that's a dive – I didn't touch him!' Trent tried to protest, but the referee had already made his decision. Boultam stepped up and scored from the spot. *1–1!*

After that 'foul', Trent found himself back on the bench, for both the 1–0 win over Ireland and the 1–0 defeat to Russia. Nooooo – there was nothing he could do; England had been knocked out in the quarter-finals!

But fortunately, their World Cup chances weren't over just yet. With a win against Spain in the play-offs, they could still qualify. For the big game, Trent was back in midfield, alongside Tom and Herbie. Together, they stopped the skilful Spaniards from scoring, but sadly, England couldn't grab a goal of their own either. One of their best chances fell to Trent, but for once, he failed to hit the target. With the score still at 0–0, it was time for penalties!

By then, Trent had been taken off, so all he could do was cheer from the bench as each of his teammates stepped up… and scored: 5–3 – England were going to Chile, after all!

'Hurraaaaay!' the players roared as they raced over to hug their goalkeeper hero, Will Huffer. 'World Cup, here we come!'

Back at the Liverpool academy, Trent and Herbie counted down the days until their next international adventure. This tournament was going to be even tougher because England would be competing against the best teams in the whole world – Brazil, Argentina, Nigeria, Mexico, and South Korea, as well as Germany,

Belgium and France. But Trent was looking forward to the challenge – that's what football was all about.

'Bring it on!' he thought to himself as he waved goodbye to his family at the airport.

Trent and his England teammates knew that the Under-17 World Cup had been the making of so many brilliant young players: Cesc Fàbregas and David Silva in 2003, Toni Kroos in 2007, Kelechi Iheanacho in 2013. So, would one of them be next to win the Golden Ball?

That would be hard for Trent to achieve, especially from the England bench. That's where he sat for the whole of their disappointing 1–1 draw with Guinea.

'How did we not win that?' he groaned at the final whistle, shaking out his fresh, restless legs. 'We had so many chances to score!'

Watching from the sidelines was the worst. All Trent wanted to do was play, and in their second match, he got his wish, against the mighty Brazil. If his team lost, their World Cup journey could soon be over. Wow, the pressure was really on for him to perform.

Trent and Herbie ran and ran at the heart of the

England midfield, battling for every ball and then sending it forward to the strikers. For the first sixty minutes, the game was going exactly according to plan. The score was still 0–0, which would be a great result against one of the best teams in the world. But then, out of nowhere, disaster struck.

As the ball dropped on the edge of the England box, Kazaiah Sterling went in for a challenge with one of the opposition midfielders. It looked like a fair, 50-50 tackle but not according to the referee, who decided it was a foul by Kazaiah. And up stepped Leandrinho to fire the free kick in off the post. *1–0 to Brazil!*

As the ball landed in the back of the England net, Trent's shoulders slumped a little. Nooooo, not after all their hard work! Football could be a really cruel game sometimes. But after a quick moment of moaning, he picked himself up again. There was no point in their feeling sorry for themselves; they had to think positively.

'Come on, lads!' Trent shouted to his teammates, trying to lift their spirits. 'We've still got plenty of time to equalise!'

But sadly, there was no way back for them against a strong Brazil defence. Arghh, it was so gutting to lose 1–0 like that. They had definitely deserved to take more than one point from their first two games, but now, England had to switch their focus to their must-win match against South Korea. Otherwise they would be out of the World Cup.

Trent hoped that he had done enough to keep his place in the team, but no, he found himself back on the bench again. And he stayed there all game long, as England attacked and attacked, but failed to score the goal they needed. It finished 0–0 – not good enough, unfortunately.

Oh well – Trent's Under-17 World Cup experience may have come to an end, but he could still return home with happy memories and no regrets. He had done his best for England and, as his coaches always told him, disappointments were all part of the learning process. Plus, hopefully, there would be more international opportunities ahead.

CHAPTER 11

RIGHT BACK, RIGHT TIME

Back at Liverpool, Trent focused on fighting his way into the first team, one step at a time, starting with winning a regular spot in the Under-18s side.

'Honestly, I'll play anywhere!' Trent told his new coach, Neil Critchley.

And he meant it. As much as he loved the Number 6 role that Lijnders had given him for the Under-16s, Trent knew that central midfield was the most popular and competitive area. He wasn't even playing for the Under-23s yet, so his chances of breaking into the Liverpool first team in that position? Almost impossible, even with Stevie G's support!

But with his talent, ambition, and athleticism,

Trent had already proved that he could play all over the pitch. So, why not move back out on to the wing for a while to get more game-time? He could always return to his favourite Number 6 role later, but for now, he needed to do what was right for the team, and for his Liverpool career.

'Good lad, you'll go far with an attitude like that!' Critchley said, putting him straight into the starting line-up as a right winger.

Although Alex Inglethorpe, the club's Academy Director, agreed wholeheartedly about Trent's tremendous attitude, he disagreed about the best position for him to play. The boy was fast, and he could cross the ball well, but he certainly wasn't a natural winger. He didn't have the silky skills to dribble past defenders; that just wasn't his style. No, instead Trent's game was all about work-rate – non-stop running, tackling, and passing. So, if he wanted to make it into the Liverpool first team, then maybe right-back might be a faster route to take...

'Right-back?' Trent repeated with surprise when they met up to discuss his future.

'Think about it, kid. Right now, who do Liverpool have in that position?'

Well, their new first choice right-back was Nathaniel Clyne, who had recently signed from Southampton. He was an England international and one of the best in the Premier League. But with Glen Johnson now gone, Liverpool's back-up right-backs weren't much older than Trent, and they certainly weren't any better. Of course, he would have to work hard to improve his defending, but he had been a centre-back once upon a time. And there was no doubt that Trent had more attacking quality than Andre Wisdom, Jon Flanagan, or Connor Randall.

'Remember, full-back isn't the boring position that it used to be,' Inglethorpe continued. 'Look at players like Ashley Cole, Patrice Evra, Kyle Walker – they bomb up and down their flank all game long!'

It was true, those guys did as much attacking as defending, if not more! They were key players for their clubs at both ends of the pitch. The more Trent thought about the idea of becoming a right-back, the more excited he grew. Yes, he would have a lot to learn, but he was willing to do anything to play for Liverpool.

Inglethorpe had one last incentive up his sleeve: 'Do you know what position Steven Gerrard played in his first Premier League game? Right-back!'

Trent didn't need any more convincing. 'I'm in!' he told his academy director eagerly.

But Trent didn't just turn into a top right-back overnight. No, it took hours and extra-hours on the training field, plus plenty of match experience too. Some good, some bad:

'Well tracked back, Trent!'

'No, don't dive in!'

'That's it, show him onto his weaker foot!'

'Come on, that was your man, Trent!'

'What a tackle, mate!'

'Kid, watch the overlap!'

But really, all experience was good experience because it was helping Trent to become a better right-back.

'Excellent performance, lad,' his Under-18s coach, Critchley, encouraged him. 'You look like you've been playing there all your life!'

The next step for Trent would be to test himself at Under-23 level, against better, stronger attackers. He couldn't wait. That was all he was thinking about ahead of the 2015–16 campaign, but that all changed when he got a surprise call-up to train with the first team during preseason.

Woah, really?! Trent couldn't believe it. It wasn't long ago that he was standing on bins with his brothers to spy on his heroes at Melwood, and now, he would be one of those lucky Liverpool players! It seemed too good to be true.

Why him? 'Because you're a right-back at the right time!' Inglethorpe said with a smile. Their plan was working perfectly.

But what if Trent wasn't ready? What if he made a bad mistake and Rodgers never invited him back? No, he couldn't think like that. He had to stay calm and confident.

'Hey, you'll be great,' the academy director reassured him. 'Just play your natural game and everything will be fine.'

That first day at training was like the first day at

a new school; no, actually, it was way more nerve-wracking! Trent didn't know what to do or where to go as he entered the first team changing room. Where was he supposed to sit? Was he supposed to speak or stay quiet? He was surrounded by experienced international footballers, like Philippe Coutinho, Jordan Henderson and Kolo Touré. Did he really belong here?

'Hi kid, how's it going?' Trent heard someone ask as he put his kitbag down. As he looked up, he saw that it was Henderson – the Liverpool captain – and he was speaking to him!

'Y-yeah good, th-thanks.'

'You're Trent Arnold, right?'

He nodded.

'Stevie told us all about ya. He says you're going to be a star.'

After that, Trent was totally lost for words. The Liverpool captain had heard of him?! Now, the pressure was really on to perform.

But Trent wasn't going to 'bottle it' and waste his big first-team opportunity. No, he was too determined and competitive to do that. It took a few training sessions for him to settle in properly, but eventually he forgot that he was playing with his heroes. It was just football and he was good at that. Very good indeed.

'Great work, Trent!'

On 2 August, Liverpool took on Swindon Town in their final preseason friendly. On Rodgers's teamsheet that day, there were lots of famous footballers: Touré, Mamadou Sakho, Emre Can, Lucas Leiva, plus expensive new forwards Christian Benteke and Roberto Firmino...

But in amongst them all, there was an unknown name at right-back: Trent Alexander-Arnold.

CHAPTER 12

DEBUTS AT THE DEEP END

Trent's first game for the Liverpool first team lasted fifty-eight minutes. As he walked off the field at the County Ground, he felt satisfied with his performance. His team were on track to keep a clean sheet and they were winning 1–0 thanks to a brilliant Christian Benteke chest and volley. Although Trent hadn't been able to do much attacking, he had been dependable in defence. That would do for now.

'A solid, if unspectacular, display,' Trent's dad Michael read out from the 'This is Anfield' website. '6.5 out of 10.'

'Nah, I'd have given you a 5!' Tyler joked. He was very proud of his brother, even if he preferred not to show it.

Yes, 6.5 out of 10 was a very solid start to Trent's Liverpool career. Not bad for a sixteen-year-old, who had only fairly recently become a right-back!

Trent spent the rest of the 2015–16 season training with the first team, while getting more valuable game-time with the Under-18s. He also made his debut for the Under-23s, but that turned out to be a very difficult afternoon indeed. The Liverpool defence just couldn't cope with Manchester City's dangerous attack, and they lost 3–0.

After that match, the Under-23s coach, Michael Beale, put an arm around Trent's shoulder. 'Unlucky, lad, that was a tough test today. Keep your head up and keep working hard. You'll bounce back better than ever.'

For Trent, that trouncing against Manchester City was a timely reminder that he still had a long way to go, especially if he wanted to be a top defender. Each week, he tried to learn as much as he could from watching Nathaniel Clyne up close in training, and then put it into practice on the pitch for the Under-18s.

Match after match, Trent could feel himself making progress. Speed, strength, aggression, awareness – he polished every aspect of his game until he had it all. Yes, he was a real right-back now and he was building up nicely towards what he hoped would be his breakthrough year – 2016–17. He would be playing for the Under-23s squad permanently now and if he could start the new season well, who knew what might happen…

In his first four games in the Premier League 2, Trent was on fire, scoring two and setting up two. He did his job in defence and then attacked as often as he could. Against Sunderland, he raced forward, controlled a long ball beautifully, nutmegged the left-back once and then beat him again, before smashing a shot into the top corner of the net.

Goooooooooooooooooooaaaaaaaaaaaaaaaaaalllllllllllll llllllllllllll!!!!!!!!!!!!!!!!!!!

It was an absolute wondergoal - what ridiculous skills from a right-back! With technique like that, Trent was certainly ready for the next step-up. It was time for him to make his official Liverpool first team debut.

So, would he come on for a few minutes at the end of a Premier League match? No – the new manager, Jürgen Klopp, decided to throw him straight in at the deep end: in the starting line-up for their EFL Cup Fourth Round tie against Tottenham... at Anfield!

Trent hadn't been expecting to play at all, but on the day before the game, as the Liverpool manager went through the team formation, there he was at right-back! What? Was he ready for this? He would have to be! It was a total shock but at least there wasn't much time for him to panic. And it helped that he wasn't the only youngster in the Starting XI – Ovie Ejaria would also be playing in midfield. So they could go through this nerve-wracking experience together...

'Don't worry, you'll be great today,' Klopp told them both before kick-off to try and calm them down. 'I believe in you both – just go out there and play!'

Fortunately, Trent wouldn't be up against Harry Kane and Dele Alli on his senior debut, but he would still have to defend against Tottenham's new £20million striker, Vincent Janssen, plus their tricky young wingers, Josh Onomah and Georges-Kevin N'Koudou. All in front of 53,000 fans.

'You can do this,' Trent told himself, as he listened to the Anfield roar.

Right from kick-off, Liverpool's new Number 66 attacked with energy and confidence. Trent was nervous but excited, and eager to impress Klopp, along with the whole Alexander-Arnold family watching in the stands. In only the third minute of the match, he dribbled his way into the Tottenham box and tried to slip a pass through to Daniel Sturridge.

'Unlucky, Trent – right idea!' the Liverpool striker shouted.

Five minutes later, Daniel tapped in the opening goal, and who was his nearest teammate? Trent! Yes, from right-back, he had sprinted all the way into the six-yard box to join the attack.

'Come on!' Trent cheered, leaping high into the Anfield air. It was looking like a dream debut so far.

'Don't forget about defending, though,' he told himself as he jogged back to the halfway line. All those forward runs were fine, as long as he didn't

get caught out of position and give away a goal.
That would be a disaster on his Liverpool debut.

And so would a red card. But in the twenty-fifth
minute, Trent flew into a reckless tackle on the
Tottenham left-back, Ben Davies. He was aiming for
the ball, but he missed and got the man instead.

'REF!' the Spurs players raced over to complain.

Uh oh, Trent was in trouble. He could see the
referee reaching into his pocket, but what colour
would the card be? Phew, only a yellow! He was a
lucky boy. Okay, that was his warning – it was time
for him to calm down and focus.

Trent bounced back well from his booking and
by the time he came off in the sixty-eighth minute,
Liverpool were 2–0 up and cruising to a comfortable
victory.

'Well played, mate!' Nathaniel shouted as he ran
on to replace him.

Klopp was next to congratulate him. 'Great game,
kid!'

Trent couldn't stop smiling after that. His team
was winning, and his manager was impressed – job

done! Onto the next round...

He kept his place for the quarter-finals against Leeds United and this time, he even proved to be Liverpool's matchwinner. The score was 0–0 with fifteen minutes to go when Trent chested the ball down and looked up to cross it in. Most young right-backs would have just curled it into the box and hoped for the best, but not him. He had the brilliant football brain to do better than that. Trent spotted Divock Origi making a run between the centre-backs and delivered the perfect ball. *1–0!*

'Get in!' Trent roared, racing over to celebrate with Divock and the Liverpool fans behind the goal.

He was definitely part of the first team now. After that, Klopp put him on the bench for four league games in a row, bringing him on for the last minute against Middlesbrough. Trent now had his first Premier League appearance, and his full debut came a few weeks later... away at Old Trafford.

Manchester United vs Liverpool – it was probably the biggest game in the whole of English football. Klopp needed to put out his best possible team, but in the days leading up to the match, it became clear that Nathaniel wouldn't be fit to play. So, who would take his place? The Liverpool manager thought about playing Alberto Moreno at left-back and moving James Milner to the right, but no, in the end, he decided to trust Trent. Yes, he was young and inexperienced, but he could handle the pressure of taking on Manchester United – in particular, Anthony Martial, one of the most exciting young forwards in the world.

'Don't let him cut inside, don't let him cut inside,' Trent kept telling himself as the Frenchman dribbled forward on the attack.

Martial was playing on the left wing for United, but it was his right foot that Liverpool were worried about. It wasn't easy to stop him, but Trent stuck to his task brilliantly and got better and better as the game went on. In the second half, he kept Martial so quiet that José Mourinho took him off after sixty-five minutes. Another job well done.

'Alexander-Arnold will never forget this day – there will be plenty more to come in a Liverpool shirt,' Trent's dad Michael read out from the 'This is Anfield' website. '7 out of 10.'

Tyler laughed. 'See, bro – you're getting better!'

CHAPTER 13

SHOOTING ENGLAND TO THE EUROS

For Trent, 2016–17 was exactly the breakthrough season that he had been hoping for, both for club and country. Thanks to the move from central midfield to right-back, he was now a regular starter for the England Under-19s. The coach, Keith Downing, loved his attacking style and encouraged him to get forward at every opportunity. It was something that their opponents wouldn't be expecting.

'You'll need to do a bit of defending too, though!' Downing added with a smile.

Trent didn't mind that; he loved both sides of the right-back role. But attacking was what he did best, and for the England Under-19s, he took full advantage of his extra freedom.

GOAL! GOAL! Trent started by scoring two in a friendly against Croatia – a long-range strike and then a penalty kick.

From there, his fine form continued during England's qualifiers for Euro 2017:

GOAL! GOAL! Trent claimed both of his team's goals against Wales, even if the first did take a deflection.

'No way is that an own goal,' he argued with Tom Davies afterwards. 'My shot was going in anyway!'

GOAL! He scored another from the spot against Greece.

ASSIST! He dribbled his way past three Norway defenders, before pulling a perfect ball back for Mason Mount to tap in.

'Yes, Trent!' Mason cheered, giving his teammate a hug.

But England's exciting right-back saved his best performance for their next game against Spain. In the ninth minute, Trent got the ball and raced forward down the wing. Marc Cucurella, Spain's left-back, was expecting him to cross it, but instead, he cleverly cut inside and into the penalty area. On his weaker foot, Trent faked as if he was aiming for the far corner, but then squeezed his shot in at the near post instead. *1–0!*

Goooooooooooooooooooooaaaaaaaaaaaaaaaaalllllllllllll llllllllllllllll!!!!!!!!!!!!!!!!!!!!

'Yesssss!' Trent roared punching the air with both fists. Everything about the goal had been brilliant: the speed, the skill, the shot, but especially the quick thinking. He had made the Spanish defence look like fools!

And in the second half, he did it again. When the left winger, Fran García, stopped him from dribbling down the line, Trent just took a different route instead. In a flash, he burst infield, past García and into the box, where Cucurella flew in to make a reckless foul. Penalty to England!

Trent picked himself up and took the spot-kick himself. After a few short steps, he blasted the ball into the net, sending the keeper the wrong way. *2–0!*

Goooooooooooooaaaaaaaaaaaalllllllllllllll!!!!!!!!!!!!

Another game, another two goals for England's remarkable right-back. Trent was simply unstoppable, and thanks to him, they were off to Euro 2017!

'And we're going to win it!' he declared confidently as the team celebrated their success at St George's Park.

However, as the big tournament approached, Trent had a difficult decision to make. Should he go and play for the England Under-19s at Euro 2017 or stay at Liverpool for preseason training? Klopp wanted to work with his squad throughout the summer and get them super-fit for the new season. That included Trent. He had already made twelve appearances for the first team and the Liverpool manager had promised that he would play a lot more during the 2017–18 campaign.

'What if I go to Georgia and get an injury?' Trent worried. 'I could lose my place at Liverpool!'

No, he couldn't let that happen. It wasn't easy saying no to England, but he decided to put club football first for now. His international adventures would just have to wait.

Even without their remarkable right back, the England Under-19s still won Euro 2017, beating Portugal 2–1 in the final. Watching it on TV at home after training, Trent was delighted for his teammates, but at the same time, he couldn't help thinking, 'That could have been me!'

Had he made the wrong decision by staying loyal to Liverpool? Only time would tell, but hopefully, Trent's gamble was going to pay off during the 2017–18 season.

CHAPTER 14

SET-PIECE SKILLS
AND MORE

'Your turn, Trent. Go on, lad!'

In the early days, Trent hadn't felt that comfortable around the Liverpool first team. The other guys seemed so much older and wiser and better than him. He didn't feel like he'd done enough yet to deserve their respect. So instead, he had stuck with the players his own age, like Ovie, Marko Grujić, Harry Wilson and Ben Woodburn.

But one year on, Trent was really starting to feel like he belonged amongst the big boys. The Liverpool players had welcomed in, even letting him join the free-kick crew.

Trent was used to taking penalties and corners,

and he loved a long pass like Stevie G, but he had never thought much about free kicks before. So, at first, he mostly watched and learned from the other members of the group: Philippe Coutinho, Emre Can, Alberto Moreno and Gini Wijnaldum.

Each and every one of them had a different technique – some went for curl and curve, others went for dip and swerve. Trent tried all kinds of things until eventually he found out what worked best for him: whip.

BANG!... GOAL!

'Nice one, mate – you're getting really good at that!'

'Thanks, Gini!'

Trent wasn't improving by accident; again, it was all about practice, practice, practice. Once he started working on something, he didn't stop.

Klopp was pleased to see his young right-back settling into the squad. That was an important part of his progress as a first-team player. The Liverpool manager was a big fan of Trent's football talent, but he wanted him to be a bit louder and more confident.

'Don't be shy to speak up,' Klopp told Trent at training. 'You've got to be brave and believe in yourself – you're a key part of our squad now.'

In fact, when Liverpool announced their team for their first game of the 2017–18 season, Trent was there in the new selection for the starting line-up, and with Nathaniel out injured until at least Christmas, so he was the first-choice full back, at least for now – at the age of only eighteen.

What an opportunity! Trent was a right-back at the right time, but could he now go on and really make the most of his chance? It was an exciting new era for Liverpool Football Club, and he was desperate to be a part of it. Player by player, position by position, Klopp was building an unbelievable team. They now had Mohamed Salah, Sadio Mané and Roberto Firmino in attack, Hendo and Gini in midfield, and if he kept impressing and improving, Trent in defence.

'Yes, I'm here to stay!' he told himself determinedly.

In order to compete in the Champions League group stage, Liverpool would first have to beat Hoffenheim. The Germans were the better team for much of the first half, but all of a sudden, Sadio broke forward on the counterattack. He skipped past the first tackle, but the second one clipped his ankle. *Free kick to Liverpool!*

The ball was in a good shooting position and Philippe wasn't playing, so the other members of the free-kick crew gathered around it.

'Let me take it!' Alberto argued confidently.

'No, me!' added Emre.

It was Hendo who had the final say: 'No, Trent is having this one.'

Next to him, Gini nodded in agreement. They knew what he could do; he just needed a little push.

Really? Well, okay. If his captain said so! Trent placed the ball down, took three steps back and then focused on the target. First, he would have to get his shot past the seven Hoffenheim players in the wall, and then past the keeper on the line. He would have to hit it perfectly.

'Come on, you can do this,' Trent told himself.

When the referee's whistle blew, he ran up and *BANG!* He whipped the ball up over the middle of the wall and then watched as it dipped down into the bottom corner. The Hoffenheim keeper didn't even move. *1–0!*

Goooooooooooooooooooaaaaaaaaaaaaaaaaalllllllllllll llllllllllllll!!!!!!!!!!!!!!!!!!!!!

Trent was off the mark for Liverpool and what a way to do it – with a free kick in the first game of the new season! He raced away to celebrate by the corner flag, with the rest of the crew following close behind.

'What a beauty!' screamed Alberto.

'Great goal!' cried Emre.

'That was class, mate!' yelled Hendo. 'We knew you could do it!'

Thanks to Trent, Liverpool were on their way to the Champions League group stage. And when they got there, the good times continued.

GOAL! Trent scored the last goal as they thrashed Maribor 7–0 away in Slovenia. His shot took a big deflection off a defender, but so what? He was still claiming it.

'Are you sure your strike was on target, mate?' James joked. 'It looked like it was heading wide to me...'

'Of course, it was going in, Milly!' he replied with

a cheeky grin.

ASSIST! At home at Anfield, Trent tormented Maribor again. Early in the second half, he curled a teasing cross towards Mo, who flicked the ball brilliantly past the keeper. 1–0!

'Thanks, mate!' his Egyptian teammate shouted as they celebrated the goal together.

With each magical European performance, Trent was becoming more and more important to the Liverpool team. Thanks to his early days in central midfield, he had the vision and ability to pick out extraordinary passes. He created so many chances when he raced forward from right back and his final ball was consistently fantastic.

Klopp had to keep reminding himself that Trent was still only a teenager. He tried his best to look after his young star and not give him too much game-time. So, in the Premier League, it was often Joe Gomez who started at right-back instead, unless the Liverpool manager wanted a more attacking option.

When they were at home to Swansea City, who were bottom of the league, it was the perfect game for Trent and his fellow full back, Andy Robertson, to fly up the wings to support the Liverpool attack.

In the first half, Andy hit a swerving shot that whistled just wide of the post.

'Unlucky Robbo,' Trent called out to his teammate. They got on really well and had lots of fun together. 'Don't worry, I'll show you how it's done!'

It took a while for an opportunity to arrive, but when it did, he took it beautifully. Midway through the second half, a Swansea defender headed a cross away, but only as far as the edge of the area. In a flash, Trent raced in to beat the winger to the ball. With his first touch, he poked it forward and with his second, he smashed it into the top corner. 3–0!

Goooooooooooooooooooooaaaaaaaaaaaaaaaaaallllllllllll llllllllllllll!!!!!!!!!!!!!!!!!!!!

'Come on!' Trent roared, loud and proud, as he slid towards the fans on his knees.

Step aside, Stevie G – Liverpool had a new homegrown hero.

CHAPTER 15

FIGHTING TO STAY FIRST CHOICE

There seemed to be no stopping Trent and his rapid rise to the top. Even the news that Nathaniel was finally ready to return to training wasn't going to hold him back. No, he had earned his place in the team and he wasn't going to let anyone take it away. Trent and Andy were Liverpool's first-choice full backs now.

Yes, they both loved to attack, but Klopp trusted them to defend too, even in the biggest Premier League games. Trent had already played well once away at Old Trafford, so why couldn't he do it again?

This time, there was no Martial in the Manchester United line-up, but Trent would be up against

Marcus Rashford instead, another skilful young forward with explosive speed.

'Bring it on!' Trent thought confidently. He loved testing himself against the best.

However, for once, it was a test that he failed.

United had a plan and it worked perfectly. In the fourteenth minute, their striker, Romelu Lukaku, jumped up and won the flick-on. As the ball bounced down, Rashford beat Trent to it and then raced away into the Liverpool penalty area.

Trent sprinted back as fast as he could and tried to stop him, but Rashford fooled him with a Ronaldo chop and then fired a shot into the far corner. *1–0 to Manchester United!*

As Old Trafford went wild, Trent stood there, staring down at the grass, with nowhere to hide. It was a brilliant solo goal, but how had he let Rashford win the ball in the first place?! He was furious with himself.

'Come on, heads up!' Liverpool's new centre-back, Virgil van Dijk, called out to him. 'Keep going!'

But before they could get back in the game,

Rashford scored a second time. Again, Lukaku won the header and this time, he passed it through to Alexis Sánchez. Trent raced across to try and tackle the Chilean, but by doing that, he left Rashford free in lots of space. When the ball bounced out to him, there was nothing Trent could do. It was too late. 2–0!

'Noooo!' he groaned as his shoulders slumped. Another goal, another error.

Liverpool fought back in the second half, but it still finished 2–1 to United. For Trent, it was an especially tough defeat to take. He had lost his battle and his team had lost the match. Rashford had got the better of him and he hated that. It was a horrible feeling, the worst in football.

'Hey, these things happen,' Klopp tried to reassure him. 'It's how you react that's important.'

All Trent could do was move on and learn from his mistakes. In the days after the Manchester United match, he went through every detail over and over again in order to understand his errors. To be a top right-back, he had to be brilliant at both defending and attacking. One out of two was not enough, not at the elite level. He talked things through with his manager and then went to see his old academy director too.

Trent trusted Alex Inglethorpe to always tell him the truth, no matter how painful that might be. He needed honesty and he needed answers. What had gone wrong and how could he make sure that it didn't happen again? How could he become a better defender? He was willing to do whatever it took to improve and turn his one weakness into another strength.

'Do you remember what we used to tell you at the Academy when you first moved to right back?' Inglethorpe asked him. 'Make it a competition. That duel between you and the winger is a battle and you've got to win it. No matter who they are or what they do, you can't let him beat you. Come on, I know how competitive you are!'

Trent nodded his head and even allowed himself a little smile. 'Thanks Coach, I'll work on that.'

There was no instant fix, however. It took time and effort, and there were more errors along the way. Unfortunately for Trent, his next Premier

League opponent was Wilfried Zaha. He was as quick as Rashford and even more skilful, so Crystal Palace just copied Manchester United's plan. And it worked. Again and again, Zaha got in behind Trent, causing him all kinds of trouble, until eventually, it led to a goal. The Liverpool keeper, Loris Karius, came out and clattered into him. *Penalty – 1–0 to Palace!*

'Not again!' Trent groaned. He had to do better than that. 'Focus!'

This time, Liverpool managed to bounce back and win the game, thanks to goals from Sadio and Mo. Phew! But Trent knew that he was still in trouble. He couldn't keep making defensive mistakes, otherwise Klopp would have to find a new right-back to replace him. He had a fight on his hands if he wanted to remain first choice. It was time to push himself harder than ever.

Four days later, Liverpool faced their Premier League rivals, Manchester City, in the Champions League quarter-finals. It was a massive clash, where any mistakes could prove incredibly costly. Plus, City's left winger, Leroy Sané, was lightning-quick and lethal in front of goal. Uh oh…

So, would Klopp play it safe and pick a more reliable right-back instead – like Nathaniel or James? No, the Liverpool manager believed in Trent and he trusted him to prove his critics wrong. Of course, he could defend!

Trent had been taught a harsh lesson over the last few weeks, but he was ready to put things right. He did lots of homework on Sané; he wasn't going to underestimate a winger ever again. The German was very talented, but he was also very left-footed. That meant that if he ever cut inside, he would try to cut back out again. Trent would have to watch out for that.

In the first leg at Anfield, Trent put on one of his best performances for Liverpool. He beat Sané to every ball and stopped him every time he tried to twist and turn his way down the wing.

'Well done, lad!' the Liverpool fans urged him on.

Trent was so fired up for the big European night that nothing and no-one was going to get past him. He was determined to reach the Champions League Final and win it, just like his childhood heroes in

2005. As the game went on, Trent's confidence grew and grew. By pushing further forward, he forced Sané to track back. But first and foremost, he got his defensive work done.

At the final whistle, Trent punched the air with passion and joy. He had won his battle and his team had won the match 3–0. What a victory! Although there was still a second leg to come, he had to stop and savour the moment because football feelings didn't get much sweeter than this. After a difficult few weeks, he had fought back brilliantly. He deserved all of the praise he got.

'Trent had a fantastic game,' said Klopp in every interview.

'The kid came good today,' declared Rio Ferdinand on TV.

CHAPTER 16

2018: A CHAMPIONS LEAGUE FINAL TO FORGET

Six days later, Liverpool faced Manchester City again, for the second leg, and when they won 2–1, the football world was raving about Trent Alexander-Arnold's performance. After his horror show against Rashford, he had really turned things around by keeping Sané quiet in the Champions League quarter-finals.

Sitting alongside Rio Ferdinand in the TV studio was a Liverpool legend who knew all about Trent's ability:

'If you look at his age and who he was up against,' Steven Gerrard argued, 'he has to be the star man over the two legs.'

It was great to hear that from his hero, but Trent wasn't getting carried away with the compliments. Instead, he moved straight on to the next challenge. Liverpool were through to their first Champions League semi-final since 2005. Could they now go all the way and win the trophy again? The excitement was building amongst the club's supporters, but the players were taking things one step at a time. Although they were in great form and full of confidence, they couldn't let their focus slip. Not until the trophy was theirs.

Next up: Roma. Against his old team, Mo was Liverpool's man of the match, scoring two and setting up two more for Sadio and Roberto. On the counterattack, their front three were so hard to stop. The first leg finished 5–2 – surely, they were already through to the final?

No – any celebrations were premature. In the second half of the second leg, Liverpool almost threw it all away. At 7–3 up, they lost their focus and allowed Roma to fight back – 7–4, 7–5, 7–6! Fortunately for Trent and his teammates, the final whistle went before the Italians could score again.

Trent's first feeling was relief. It was only later
that the news really sunk in. At the age of nineteen,
he was about to follow in the footsteps of his heroes
and play in a Champions League Final. It was beyond
his wildest childhood dreams.

'Well done!' Klopp congratulated his players. 'But
if we defend like that against Real Madrid, Ronaldo
is going to destroy us!'

And it wasn't just Ronaldo they had to worry
about; the Spanish giants had quality players in
every position. Sergio Ramos and Raphaël Varane in
defence; Toni Kroos and Luka Modrić in midfield;
and then Isco, Gareth Bale and Karim Benzema
in attack. Wow, no wonder Real had won the
Champions League for the last two years in a row!

But as the final kicked off in Kiev, Liverpool were
prepared for the big occasion, and they played
without fear. In the seventh minute, Trent raced
all the way into the Real Madrid penalty area and
almost beat Keylor Navas to the bouncing ball. So
close! Five minutes later, he flew forward again to

deliver a dangerous cross towards Sadio, which Navas punched away just in time.

'Keep going!' Klopp clapped and cheered.

Trent was busy at the back too. Ronaldo, Isco and Benzema were all taking it in turns to drift over to the left and team up with Marcelo, who was playing more like a winger than a defender.

'I need some help here!' Trent called out to his teammates.

The exciting, end-to-end football lasted until the twenty-fifth minute, when disaster struck for Liverpool. As Ramos wrestled Mo to the ground, he landed awkwardly on his left shoulder. Arghhh! He tried his best to play on, but he couldn't – it was too painful.

That was Liverpool's first bit of bad luck, followed by another early in the second half. As Loris went to roll the ball out to Dejan Lovren, Benzema stretched out a leg to block it. Nooooo! Trent and his teammates watched in horror and disbelief as the ball trickled backwards, over their goal-line. *1–0 to Real Madrid!*

It would take more than one freak mistake to stop this tough new Liverpool team, though. Four minutes later, they were level, thanks to Sadio's strike. 1–1 – game on!

'Focus, lads!' Hendo shouted as the whole team celebrated together. 'Let's win this now!'

There was heartbreak to come, however. Trent did the right thing by showing Marcelo onto his weaker right foot, but the Brazilian still managed to cross the ball in. And up jumped Real Madrid's substitute, Gareth Bale, to score a breathtaking bicycle-kick. *2–1!*

Trent stopped still and stared as the ball landed in the net. He couldn't believe what he had just seen. Had Bale really meant to do that? As brilliant as the strike was, it was such bad luck for Liverpool.

And there was still more to come. With ten minutes to go, Bale hit a swerving shot and it slipped straight through Loris' gloves. *3–1!*

Game over. Trent sank to his knees in despair. What a horrible way to lose! There was no way back for Liverpool now.

After the final whistle, Trent sat there for ages

on the grass, just staring into space. He didn't
know what else to do. It was gutting, by far the
worst feeling he'd ever experienced in football.
He had come so close to achieving his Champions
League dream. To miss out like that, in such strange
circumstances… it was absolutely devastating. He
felt like he had let everyone down – his teammates,
his family, the fans, the whole city of Liverpool.

'Hey, you played so well tonight,' Klopp said as he
came over to comfort him. 'You should be so proud
of that performance. I know it hurts but we'll be
back, I promise, and next time we'll win!'

Eventually Trent managed to pick himself up
and collect his runners-up medal, even if it wasn't
the one he wanted. As he walked away, past the
trophy, he was in absolute agony. There was only one
thing that could heal his heartbreak – winning the
Champions League next year.

CHAPTER 17

WORLD CUP 2018

It was a good thing that Trent didn't have a long summer holiday to sit around and dwell on that night in Kiev. Instead, he was forced to move on and focus on his next challenge – winning the 2018 World Cup with England.

'No way, this must be a wind-up!' That was Trent's first thought when he got the call from the national team manager, Gareth Southgate. After all, he was still only nineteen years old, and he hadn't even made his senior debut yet. So why would he be in the England World Cup squad?

'When we pick young players, it's not just because they are young,' Southgate explained to the media, 'it's because their performances deserve it.'

That season, Trent had played thirty-four games for Liverpool, including the greatest of them all – the Champions League final. So why not a World Cup too? He had earned this amazing opportunity, even if it did feel too good to be true.

In the special squad announcement video, he was only the third England player to be named, after Raheem Sterling and John Stones.

'ALEXANDER-ARNOLD!' voices chanted as a young fan pointed at a picture of Trent on his phone.

Wow, it was really happening; he was going to the World Cup! He could remember watching the 2006 and 2010 tournaments on TV as a young England fan, dreaming of one day playing for his country.

Well, this wasn't a dream anymore; this was real life, and Trent was determined to make the most of his opportunity. He treated his first training session like it was just a normal day at Liverpool. No nerves, no fear, just calm and confidence. When he got the ball on the edge of the area, he curled an unstoppable strike into Jordan Pickford's top corner.

Luckily, his wondergoal was caught on camera. England posted it on Twitter with a cheeky comment: 'Alright Trent, it's your first session with the squad so just keep it simple...'

No way! Simple wasn't Trent's style, and that's why Southgate had selected him for the squad. He wasn't afraid to try anything.

On 7 June, Trent made his senior England debut in a World Cup warm-up win over Costa Rica. It was a night that he would never forget and who was there to present him with his match shirt before the game? Prince William – unbelievable!

However, as the team set off for the tournament in Russia, Trent wasn't getting his hopes up about game-time. England had two other top right-backs in their squad – Kyle Walker and Kieran Trippier – so unless they both got injured, he probably wouldn't play.

Still, it was a great experience for Trent just to train with the others and be part of the squad. Right from the start, there was an amazing team spirit around the England camp. Although they played for rival Premier League clubs, they were all united when it came to representing their country and trying to win the World Cup.

'Come on, let's do this!' they cheered together like one big happy family.

It wasn't easy for Trent to sit and watch while a game of football was going on, but he did his best to support his teammates from the sidelines.

'Yes, H – you hero!' he cheered when Harry Kane scored the last-minute winner in England's first game against Tunisia.

'Well played, Hendo!' he told his Liverpool teammate as they hugged at the final whistle.

With a 6–1 thrashing of Panama, England soon made it through to the Round of 16 with a game to spare. So, would Southgate rest his stars for the final group match against Belgium and give the squad players a chance to impress? That's what Trent was hoping for, and he got his wish. Hurray, he was about to make his World Cup debut as England's right wing-back!

But, despite Trent's heroic goal-line clearance and

a series of dangerous set-pieces, the match finished England 0 Belgium 1.

'Hey, great performance today,' Southgate said, patting him on the back as he trudged off the pitch.

No, his team hadn't won, but Trent couldn't help feeling proud, as well as frustrated. He had shown that he could handle the World Cup pressure and create chances for the attackers. It was just unfortunate for him that Kieran was on fire in his position. Unlike at Liverpool, Trent was right-back, wrong time. The 2018 tournament had come a little too soon, but by 2022, he would be a first-choice starter for England. He had no doubts about that.

In the meantime, Trent would support his teammates as much as he could. When England's Round of 16 clash with Colombia went to penalties, he stood with the other substitutes on the touchline, cheering the players on.

'Bury it, Marcus!'

'Unlucky, Hendo!'

'Go on, Tripps!'

'Yes, Jordan, you hero!'

When Eric Dier scored England's winning spot-kick, Trent raced across the pitch to join the player pile-on. It was one big squad effort and together they were aiming to go all the way.

With each victory, the country's expectations grew. By the time England beat Sweden to make it through to the World Cup semi-finals, the whole nation was singing:

'It's coming home, it's coming home,
It's coming, FOOTBALL'S COMING HOME!'

When Kieran scored a free kick in the fifth minute against Croatia, the fans started thinking ahead to the World Cup final. But sadly, it wasn't to be. Despite their best efforts, England lost 2–1 in extra time.

'Absolutely devastated that our journey is over,' Trent tweeted afterwards.

It was the end of an amazing adventure, and an incredible experience for a young player like Trent. For a month, the squad had lived together as one big family, working so hard to achieve their World Cup dream. Although they hadn't brought the trophy home, they had brought football home. England had fallen in love with its national team again, and that was enough.

For now. Trent couldn't wait for World Cup 2022.

CHAPTER 18

ON THE ATTACK/ HUNGRIER THAN EVER

On the eve of the new Premier League season, Trent posted a four-word message to his fans: 'Ready. Hungrier than ever.'

Yes, 2018 had been an unbelievable year for him as a young footballer; he had played in the Champions League final and at the World Cup too. But 2019 was going to be even better because Trent was now older, stronger, and more experienced. It was time for him and his Liverpool teammates to win some trophies.

During the summer, Klopp had added four more key players to the squad: Naby Keïta and Fabinho in midfield, Xherdan Shaqiri on the wing, and most important of all, Alisson Becker in goal. They now had one of the world's best keepers to go with one of the world's best centre-backs, Virgil van Dijk.

'Great, you guys can deal with all the defending,' Trent and Robbo teased. 'We'll just fly forward on the attack!'

They were only half-joking. Liverpool's wide forwards, Mo and Sadio, loved to make runs into the middle, which meant the full backs had lots of space to get forward down the flanks and play like wingers. They had so much fun.

'I bet I get more goals and assists than you this season,' Trent told Robbo. There was nothing he loved more than a bit of friendly competition.

'You're on,' the left-back replied straight away with a smile. 'Let the battle begin!'

After twenty minutes of the opening game, Liverpool were winning 1–0, and so was Robbo. His cross set up Mo for an easy tap-in at the back post.

'Nice one, mate, but I started that move in the first place,' Trent argued with his friend after the final whistle. 'If it wasn't for my pass to Naby, then there would have been no goal. So, where's my assist? It's not fair!'

Robbo couldn't help laughing. 'Unbelievable, you're such a bad loser!'

Liverpool won all of their first five Premier League games, only conceding two goals along the way. But in the 'Battle of the Full Backs', Robbo was 2–0 up, and Trent was determined to fight back. It was time for him to go on the attack.

Against Southampton, he whipped in a wonderful corner, right onto Joël Matip's head. *2–0!*

At last, Trent had his first assist of the season. 'Game on!' he told Robbo with a grin.

A few weeks later against Fulham, Trent showed off his clever quick-thinking. While their opponents were still arguing with the referee about a disallowed goal, he launched a lethal counterattack, threading a perfect long pass through for Mo to chase. *1–0!*

Before long, it was 2–0, and this time, it was all thanks to Robbo, who curled in a lovely cross to Xherdan. Liverpool's full backs were on fire!

Trent continued his attacking form for England

against the USA. As Jadon Sancho got the ball just inside the box, he seemed to be on his own. But no,

'Yes!' Trent called out as he flew forward from right back, catching the USA winger by surprise.

The weight of the pass was perfect, so Trent didn't even take a touch to control it. *BANG!* He fired the ball hard and low into the bottom corner. The accuracy was astonishing. *2–0!*

Goooooooooooooooooooooaaaaaaaaaaaaaaaaalllllllllllll llllllllllllll!!!!!!!!!!!!!!!!!!!

Trent threw his arms out wide and then jumped high into the air. What a feeling it was to score his first international goal in front of 68,000 fans! Hopefully, there would be many more to come.

'Childhood dream: Score at Wembley for England,' Trent tweeted afterwards with a tick emoji. Although he had achieved so much already in his short career, he was still hungry for more. In fact, he was hungrier than ever.

Ten days later, Trent was back on the scoresheet again, but this time for Liverpool. When the team won a free kick late in the second half in a good

shooting position, lots of players wanted to take it –
Hendo, Mo, Gini, Roberto, James. But one by one,
they stepped away to leave it for Trent. They knew
what he could do with one whip of his right boot.

BANG!

*Goooooooooooooooooooooaaaaaaaaaaaaaaaalllllllllllll
lllllllllllll!!!!!!!!!!!!!!!!!!!!!*

The ball sailed into the net before the Watford
keeper could even try to stop it.

'What a strike!' Hendo yelled out, throwing his
arms around Trent.

Liverpool still hadn't lost a Premier League game
all season, and yet somehow, they sat two points
behind Manchester City at the top of the table. All
they could do was keep winning, starting with one
of their most important games of the season: The
Merseyside Derby.

Liverpool's record against their local rivals Everton
was very good, especially at home in front of the
Anfield roar. However, they were always tight,
competitive clashes, and three of their previous five
meetings had ended 0–0. But a draw wouldn't do this

time – not if Liverpool wanted to lift the league title.

'Come on guys, let's go!' Virgil shouted as he led his team out of the tunnel and on to the pitch for kick-off.

Trent looked as calm as ever but inside he was buzzing with excitement. The local lad from West Derby was about to play in his first proper Merseyside Derby and he couldn't wait. Klopp had brought him on as a late substitute on a couple of occasions in the past, but this time, he was on the field from the start and hopefully, he would play the full ninety minutes.

As Trent did a few last jogs and stretches, Anfield was filled with the sound of that famous Liverpool song, the one he remembered hearing on his very first trip to the stadium as a six-year-old boy:

Walk on, walk on,

With hope in your heart,

And YOU'LL NEVER WALK ALONE!

Although Trent was now Liverpool's regular right-back, the sound of that song still gave him goosebumps every time. It made him even more pumped up and ready to win the derby.

At half-time, however, the score was still 0–0.
Everton were defending deep and cutting out Trent
and Robbo's dangerous crosses from the wings.
Meanwhile, Liverpool's attackers had all missed shots
from good positions.

'Keep going!' Klopp urged his players. 'The
winning goal will come!'

But as the second-half minutes ticked by, it didn't
arrive. When Trent tried to cross it to Roberto, an
Everton defender intercepted it just in time. When
Robbo tried to cross it to Sadio, he stretched out his
leg but couldn't quite reach it.

'Ohhhhhhhh!' the Liverpool fans groaned. So
close... again! Oh no, was the Merseyside Derby
going to end in another disappointing 0–0 draw?

Klopp brought Divock Origi on as a late sub and
he hit the crossbar from Trent's curling corner-kick.
Nooooooo! Surely, that was it for Liverpool? The six
minutes of stoppage time were almost up...

It was now or never. In the final seconds, Trent
launched one last attack, one last hopeful ball

towards the crowded Everton box. Yerry Mina managed to head it away, but only as far as Virgil, who attempted an ambitious volley. As the ball sliced off his boot and looped up high into the air, Virgil turned away in disgust, thinking it was game over.

But no, everyone else at Anfield kept watching as it slowly dipped towards the goal and then bounced off Jordan Pickford's crossbar.

Both team's supporters held their breath. Which way would the ball land – out for an Everton goal kick, or back into play? This time, luck was on Liverpool's side. It bounced twice along the bar and then dropped down in the six-yard box for Divock to head it in. 1–0!

Goooooooooooooooooooooaaaaaaaaaaaaaaaalllllllllllll llllllllllllll!!!!!!!!!!!!!!!!!!!!

As the ball crossed the line, Anfield erupted with noise and emotion. What a mad moment on Merseyside – Liverpool had won the derby, after all! Klopp raced onto the pitch to celebrate with Alisson, while the rest of the players rushed over to the Kop End.

'Come on!' Trent roared with passion, right in front of the fans. It was one of the greatest moments of his entire life. Not only had Liverpool just beaten their biggest local rivals with a last-minute winner, but their Premier League title dream was still alive.

CHAPTER 19

KING OF THE ASSISTS

Trent first felt a twinge in his knee when he was warming up before the Brighton game. However, he wasn't the kind of person who worried about injuries. He was young and healthy, and Liverpool had to win. So, he played on through the pain and helped his team to a 1–0 victory. It was only afterwards as he hobbled into the physio room that he wondered if he had made things worse.

'I'm afraid you've got some ligament damage,' the club doctor told him after doing a series of checks. 'It's nothing too serious but you will need to rest for at least a few weeks.'

A few weeks?! That was a very long time in top-level football. Trent looked fearfully at the Liverpool fixture list. Okay, so he would probably miss four Premier League games, but it was possible to be back in time for the Champions League Last 16. Phew!

Thanks to lots of long, lonely hours in the gym, Trent actually only missed three league matches. He was back on the bench against Bournemouth and then into the starting line-up for the home game against Watford. Ah, it felt good to be back in action at Anfield!

Right from kick-off against Watford, Liverpool were the team on top. Trent hardly had any defending to do; it was all-out attack. In the eighth minute, he got the ball on the right wing, and after two quick touches, he was ready to deliver the cross. *WHIP!* He saw Sadio making a great run between the Watford centre-backs and picked him out perfectly. *1-0!*

Trent was back with a bang and another assist. It was his fourth of the season, but Robbo was still two ahead on six. Right, he had some catching up to do. Ten minutes later, he set up Sadio again with another curling cross. *2–0!*

'Watch out, I'm coming for you!' Trent joked with Robbo.

Liverpool's left-back did grab two assists in the second half, but only after their right-back had already completed his hat-trick. Although Mo ran up as if he was going to take the free kick, everyone knew that Trent was the set-piece specialist. *WHIP!* His delivery dropped down right onto Virgil's head; he couldn't miss. *4–0!*

'Thanks, what a ball!' the centre-back cheered as they celebrated in front of the Kop. No, Trent hadn't scored any of his team's goals, but he had created three of them with his amazing vision and accuracy. What a remarkable right-back he was! The Liverpool fans loved their local lad and to show it, they sang him a new song of his own:

The Scouser in our team,
He's Alexander-Arnold,
He's Alexander-Arnold,
He's Alexander-Arnooooold,
The Scouser in our team!

When he heard the Anfield crowd chanting his name, Trent got goosebumps all over again. What a feeling! He was living the dream of so many people, starring for his big, boyhood club – what could be better than that?

Winning a top trophy, of course! Liverpool were in fantastic form, but unfortunately for them, so were Manchester City. With eight games to go, City were one point ahead at the top of the Premier League table.

'All we can do is win every last game,' Klopp told his players, 'and hope that City slip up.'

The Liverpool team listened to their manager and followed his instructions: eight games, eight victories. And for Trent, six more assists:

BANG! He picked out Naby at the back post against Southampton. *1–1!*

PING! His quick corner caught out Cardiff and landed at Gini's right foot. *1–0!*

CHIP! He split the Huddersfield defence with a beautiful long ball to Mo. *3–0!*

WHIP! CURL! Two more incredible crosses to set

up goals for Virgil and then Mo against Newcastle.
1–0, 2–1!

'Mate, why do you have to be so competitive –
can't you just let me win for once?' Robbo joked.
They were now tied on eleven assists each.

That was just a battle going on in the background,
though. Their full focus was on the fight for the
Premier League title. There was still only one point
separating the top two teams, so it all came down
to the last day of the season.

Before kick-off, Klopp repeated the same old
message: 'First, we need to beat Wolves, and then we
can worry about whether City beat Brighton, okay?'

'Yes, Coach!'

There was a tense atmosphere at Anfield that day,
but Trent did his best to lift the mood. After a one-
two with Hendo, he delivered another excellent
cross, which flicked off a defender and fell straight
to Sadio. *1–0!*

The deflection meant that Trent couldn't claim the
assist, but that didn't matter. Winning was the most
important thing and Liverpool were on their way.

'Hurraaaaay!' A cheer went up around Anfield,
followed ten minutes later by an even louder roar.
Even the players out on the pitch could sense what had
happened: Brighton were beating City! If things stayed
the same, Liverpool would be crowned Champions…

'Come on, stay focused!' Hendo yelled out to his
teammates. Their job wasn't done yet.

It took sixty-five minutes, but at last a second
goal arrived, and Trent was at the heart of it again.
Wolves made the mistake of giving him time and
space wide on the right wing, and they paid the
price. With a quick look-up, Trent whipped one of
his trademark crosses around the centre-backs and
down onto Sadio's diving head. 2–0!

Liverpool's heroes shared a smile and a hug, but
by then, they knew that the title race was over. The
buzz around Anfield had faded completely, a clear
sign that City were now beating Brighton.

By the time the final whistle blew, Trent felt totally
deflated. As he walked around the pitch, clapping to
the crowd, he knew that he should be feeling proud
of his great performances all season. But to lose the

Premier League title by one stupid point and end up with nothing after working so hard for thirty-eight games? That was just so hard to take, especially for a life-long Liverpool fan like himself.

'Hey, I know it hurts, kid,' Klopp said, putting an arm around his shoulder, 'but we're going to use that disappointment to come back and win it next year.'

Trent nodded and tried to force a smile onto his face. As difficult as it was, he had to focus on the positives, and there were plenty of those. His total of twelve assists was the third highest in the whole Premier League that season, and he had set a new record for a defender. The Guinness World Records even gave him a special certificate.

'Unlucky mate, you came so close!' Trent teased as he showed it to Robbo.

But the biggest positive of all was that Trent's season wasn't over, and neither was his hunt for a trophy. Because against all the odds, Liverpool had battled their way back to another Champions League Final.

CHAPTER 20

2019: A CHAMPIONS LEAGUE FINAL TO REMEMBER

1 June 2019, Wanda Metropolitano Stadium, Madrid

'Onwards to Madrid!' Trent tweeted, just hours after that disappointing day against Wolves at Anfield.

Liverpool were on their way to play in their second Champions League Final in two years, and what a journey it had been to get there.

After fighting their way out of a 'Group of Death' against PSG and Napoli, Liverpool had beaten Bayern Munich comfortably and then battered Porto in the quarter-finals. Trent had played his part, setting up a goal in both first and second legs – a cross for Roberto at Anfield, and then a magical through-ball to Mo out in Portugal.

'What a pass!' the Egyptian cheered, giving Trent a high-five.

It was so far so good for Liverpool, but next up was Lionel Messi's Barcelona. Away at the Nou Camp, Trent had to watch the whole game from the bench as the Spanish Champions taught them a painful lesson. Despite a decent performance, The Reds found themselves 3–0 down at the final whistle. How had that happened? Messi, that's how! The little magician had scored two goals, including a fantastic late free kick.

Game over? Not according to Trent and his teammates. They believed they could beat anyone 4–0, even Barcelona. At Anfield, anything was possible!

Although Mo and Roberto were both out injured, Liverpool had the home crowd behind them and Trent in the right-back role. He was ready to give everything for his club, at both ends of the pitch. Assists in attack and blocks at the back – that was the plan.

It only took Liverpool six minutes to score their first goal. Hendo's shot was saved, but Divock Origi scored the rebound. *3–1!*

'Come onnnnnnn!' Trent cried out as he ran back to the halfway line. He could feel the hope building all around the stadium. The comeback was on; they could do this!

Even as the minutes ticked by without a second goal, the Liverpool players didn't panic. Thanks to Klopp, they believed in themselves. They knew that a football match could change in a flash, especially with creative players like Trent on the pitch...

Trent had been fairly quiet in the first half, but now it was time for Liverpool's King of Assists to attack. He was determined to help his team reach another Champions League final. They had unfinished business to tie up and a trophy to lift. In the fifty-fourth minute, he won the ball back on the right wing and whipped a low cross into the box, where Gini had timed his run to perfection. *BANG! – 3–2!*

And two minutes later, Gini scored again, this time from Xherdan's cross. *3–3!*

Wow, Liverpool had done it – they were level! Trent enjoyed the moment with his teammates in front of the fans, but then it was straight back to work. Their incredible comeback wasn't yet complete; they wanted to win the match before it went to extra time.

'One more goal!' Klopp signalled to his players. That's all they needed now to pull off one of the greatest fightbacks in football history.

With fifteen minutes to go, Trent raced up the wing again to win a corner-kick for Liverpool. He was about to walk away and let Xherdan take it, when he suddenly spotted Divock in space in the middle. *TING!* Trent had an amazing idea. If he took it really quickly, maybe they could catch Barcelona out... *BANG!* He whipped the ball into the box and Divock smashed it into the top corner. *4–3!*

'Trent, you're a genius!' Gini cried out as the whole city celebrated a famous victory.

So, it was no surprise that after 'The Miracle of Anfield', Liverpool were feeling quietly confident ahead of their second Champions League final in a row. If they could beat Messi's Barcelona 4–0, then surely, they could beat anyone!

Ahead of kick-off, all the signs were good. Mo and Roberto were both back from injury and they were taking on a team that they knew very well – their English rivals, Tottenham. In the Premier League that season, Liverpool had beaten them twice, 2–1 on both occasions. They also had one other important advantage over their opponents: big game experience. Trent and his teammates already knew what playing in a Champions League final was like. This time, they knew what to do and were fully prepared to win it.

'Let's do this!' Hendo shouted as he led the Liverpool team out of the tunnel.

Trent was so focused as he walked out on to the pitch that he didn't even look up as he passed the Champions League trophy. That could wait; they needed to win the match first.

After that awful night in Kiev against Real Madrid, Trent had been sure that Liverpool would make it back to the final again. But to do it the very next year? That was sooner than even he had expected.

So, could Liverpool make the most of their second chance? Yes, and they were 1–0 up before Trent had even had a touch! Within seconds of kick-off, Hendo chipped a ball over the top for Sadio to chase. With his speed, Sadio got to it first and as he tried to cross it into the box, the ball struck Moussa Sissoko on the arm.

'Handball!' Trent cried out, along with every Liverpool fan and all of his teammates.

The referee pointed to the spot straight away, and after a check with VAR, the penalty was confirmed. Up stepped Mo, who beat the keeper with ease. *1–0!*

'Get in!' Trent yelled, with one arm around Mo and the other punching the air. What a start!

And Trent almost made it 2–0 in the sixteenth minute. When Hendo's pass arrived, he found himself in lots of space on the right. So, he dribbled forward, getting closer and closer to the Tottenham goal, until eventually a defender came out to close him down. What next? Well, there was no-one in the box for the cross, so Trent took a long-range shot instead. Why not? Maybe he could catch the keeper by surprise. *BANG!* The ball skidded across the six-yard box but flew just wide of the far post.

'Ohhhhhhhh!' the Liverpool supporters groaned.

As half-time approached, it was Robbo's turn to go for goal. This time, Hugo Loris had to tip his shot over the bar. Forget the famous front three; it was Liverpool's flying full backs that Tottenham had to watch out for!

In the second half, however, Trent and Robbo concentrated on the second part of their job: defending. Liverpool wanted a clean sheet, to go with their trophy win. Tottenham attacked again and again with Harry Kane, Dele Alli and Son Heung-min, but as hard as they tried, they couldn't score. Even when they did get past the defence, they then had to get past Alisson in goal. Impossible!

Then, just when Liverpool were preparing themselves for a nervy last ten minutes, Divock scored to make it 2–0. Game over, final won!

'Yesssssss!' Trent screamed, sprinting all the way across the pitch to join in the celebrations. They had done it; they were the new Champions of Europe!

After a few more minutes of focus, it was all over. Trent sank to his knees near the halfway line and then lay there sprawled across the grass, letting the news sink in. He was a European Champion now! He had given everything and now he was exhausted. Ecstatic, but exhausted.

'Well done, mate!' he heard voices congratulating him. 'Come on, get up – let's celebrate!'

Yes, they were right – this was the best night of his life and he wanted to enjoy every moment. With the last of his energy, he picked himself up and charged towards the Liverpool fans behind the goal, feeling a rush of pure joy and passion for his local football club.

Liverpool! Liverpool! Liverpool!

It was party time for the players and supporters, and soon, it was trophy time too. With his winner's medal around his neck, Trent stood with his teammates on the stage, waiting for Hendo to do the honours.

Ohhhhhhhhhhhhhhhhhhhhhhhhh…
Hurraaaaaaaaaaaaaaaaaaaaaaaay!

Trent threw his arms high into the air as flames shot up all around them. What a feeling, what a night! The comeback against Barcelona had been brilliant, but this was even better.

Campeones, Campeones, Olé! Olé! Olé!

'Just a normal lad from Liverpool whose dream has just come true,' Trent tweeted out to his followers, alongside a photo of him lifting the Champions League trophy.

It was the greatest moment of his life and he was so glad to have his family there in Madrid to share it with him. His parents Dianne and Michael, and his brothers Tyler and Marcel – Trent couldn't have done it without their love and support. This win was for all of them. And as proud Liverpool fans, they were delighted to have the chance to hold the trophy and take photos with it.

'Hey, you better not drop it, bro!' Trent joked as they all smiled for the cameras.

After a long night of celebrations in Madrid, the players returned to England, ready for the event that Trent had been waiting years for: Liverpool's trophy bus tour. Ever since seeing his heroes go past his house in 2005, it was something that he had always dreamed of doing. And now, the team had something to show off.

Nearly a million fans filled the city streets to greet their football heroes, waving club flags and singing club songs. Wow, their Champions League success meant so much to so many people! It was a very proud and emotional day, especially for 'The Scouser in our Team'.

'What. A. Feeling,' Trent wrote on social media. 'Love this club.'

CHAPTER 21

MORE GOALS, MORE ASSISTS, MORE TROPHIES

After the highs of lifting the Champions League trophy, Trent took a few weeks off to relax and enjoy that winning feeling. But even as he sat there soaking up the summer sun, football was never far from his mind. Before long, he was thinking ahead and setting new aims for the new season. He wanted more of everything: more goals, more assists, and lots more trophies.

It was going to be a very busy season for Liverpool, with a whopping seven pieces of silverware up for grabs: the FA Community Shield, the UEFA Super Cup and the FIFA Club World Cup, as well as the FA Cup, the EFL Cup, the Champions League, and most important of all, the Premier League. That was the one that The Reds really wanted to win.

It was now thirty years since Liverpool had last been crowned Champions of England. Thirty years! That was way too long for such a world-famous football club. Last season, they had finished second, only one painful point behind Manchester City; could they bounce back and lift the title this time?

'Bring it on!' Trent was buzzing to get going again and challenge for every trophy.

Sadly, the first trophy – the FA Community Shield - went to City after extra time and penalties. Never mind, Liverpool still had six more to go, starting with the UEFA Super Cup against the Europa League winners, Chelsea.

Trent was desperate to play every minute of every match for his club, but that just wasn't possible anymore. With so many games in the schedule, Klopp had to rotate his squad to keep everyone fit. For the Super Cup in Istanbul, it was Joe who started at right-back and Trent who had to sit restlessly on the sidelines, waiting and waiting for his opportunity to shine.

At the end of ninety minutes, the two teams were still tied at 1–1 – extra time again! The Liverpool manager turned to Trent and told him to get ready.

'Yes, Boss!' he replied eagerly. He had half an hour to help The Reds to win.

But at the end of extra time, the two teams were still tied, now at 2–2 – penalties again! Klopp looked around his tired circle of players – Roberto would take one, and so would Divock and Mo. That was only three, though; they needed five for the shoot-out. Who else was ready to step up and score?

'I will!' said Fabinho,

'And I will!' said Trent. Although he hadn't taken a proper penalty since his days with the England Under-19s, his team needed him, and he was sure that he could handle the pressure. He was a big game player, after all.

But as Trent started his long walk forward, all six previous penalties had been scored. It was 3–3 - one miss and it might be all over for Liverpool. Still, he calmly and carefully placed the ball down on the spot, took five steps back and then ran up… and

SCORED! The Chelsea keeper dived the right way and got his glove on the ball, but he couldn't stop it from landing in the bottom corner.

Phew! The Liverpool fans let out a sigh of relief, but Trent didn't show any emotion. He just jogged coolly back to the half-way line to watch the rest of the shoot-out with his teammates.

Emerson scored for Chelsea. 4–4!

Mo scored for Liverpool. 5–4!

It was all up to Tammy Abraham now. He had to score… but no, Adrián, stuck out his leg and saved it. It was over – Liverpool were the UEFA Super Cup winners!

Hurraaaaaaaaay!

The players raced straight over to hug their new goalkeeping hero. Trent jumped high into the team huddle, screaming, 'ADRIÁNNNNNNN!' Liverpool were about to lift another top trophy – what a start to the new season! It was going to be a great one; Trent could just tell.

Back in the Premier League, Liverpool looked unstoppable this time around. They won all of their first eight games, opening up an eight-point lead over City already.

'Come on, that title is going to be ours!' Trent declared.

Liverpool had to take things one win at a time, though. An away trip to Chelsea was always tough, but after their Super Cup defeat, The Blues were truly out for revenge. The Reds would have to stay calm and clever.

In the fourteenth minute, Liverpool won a free kick right on the edge of the Chelsea penalty area. Mo ran up as if he was going to curl it with his left foot but at the last second, he backheeled it for Trent to strike instead with his rocket of a right foot. *BANG!* He whipped the ball around the wall and into the top corner. *1–0!*

Goooooooooooooooooooaaaaaaaaaaaaaaaalllllllllllll lllllllllllll!!!!!!!!!!!!!!!!!!!

Trent jogged towards the corner flag with a big smile on his face. He made everything look so easy. Scoring a screamer at Stamford Bridge? No problem! Fighting for lots of different trophies in one season?

Easy! He wanted to win them all.

Although Trent didn't score many more goals for his team, he was still Liverpool's King of the Assists:

one for Robbo in the Champions League against RB Salzburg,

two for Virgil in the Premier League against Brighton,

one for Sadio in the Merseyside Derby against Everton,

and one for Roberto in the FIFA Club World Cup against Monterrey.

As the Champions of Europe, Liverpool got the chance to compete against the best clubs from around the world. To win their second trophy of the season, they just had to beat the Mexican club, Monterrey, and then the Brazilian giants, Flamengo, in the final.

Two games – that didn't sound too tricky, but they were playing away in Qatar and lots of their stars were either injured or exhausted. Against Monterrey, Virgil and Joël were both missing, so Hendo had to play at centre-back. Meanwhile, Sadio, Roberto and Trent were all sitting on the bench.

Midway through the second half, Liverpool were

drawing 1–1 and Klopp had seen enough. It was time for the super subs. He brought on Sadio, then Trent, and finally Roberto, who came on with only five minutes left. They desperately needed a winner; the last thing Liverpool wanted was more extra time and penalties.

'Come on!'

In stoppage time, Mo tried his best to dribble past two defenders on the right side of the box, but there was no way through. He needed some help.

'Yes, I'm here!' Trent called out as he raced up the right wing to join the attack.

When the ball came to him, he whipped it into the box first time, but it wasn't the delivery that Monterrey were expecting. Instead of a high cross towards the crowded back post, Trent curled a low pass towards the front post, where Roberto ran in and flicked it past the keeper. *2–1!*

Phew, Trent's quick-thinking had saved the day again!

The final against Flamengo proved to be even tougher for Liverpool. The Brazilians took them all the way to extra time, but The Reds never gave up or lost their belief. Eventually, in the ninety-ninth minute, Roberto managed to score the winner. Liverpool were the 2019 FIFA Club World Cup winners!

'WORLD CHAMPIONS,' Trent tweeted joyfully to his fans.

Liverpool had their second trophy of the season, and it was still only December. Hopefully, there would be at least one more big one to come. Back-to-back Champions Leagues would be unbelievable, but Trent had his heart and mind set on winning England's top prize first.

CHAPTER 22

PREMIER LEAGUE CHAMPIONS AT LAST!

Away at Leicester on Boxing Day – could this perhaps be a match where Liverpool dropped some Premier League points?

No way! They had been so strong all season, winning 16 of their 17 games. The other game was a draw, so they hadn't lost once! No, they couldn't let their standards slip now, not until that trophy was theirs. So, just five days after winning the FIFA Club World Cup in Qatar, the Liverpool players were back on the pitch, putting in another title-winning performance.

Trent curled a beautiful cross to Roberto at the back post. *1–0!*

Milly scored from the spot. *2–0!*

Trent fizzed another ball across to Roberto. *3-0!*

It didn't matter who they played against; Liverpool were simply unstoppable!

Game over? Not quite, according to Trent. He already had two assists, but as soon as Sadio got the ball in the centre-circle, *ZOOM!* Trent raced up the right wing on another attack. His speed was incredible, like a 100-metre sprinter, even in the 79th minute of his 26th game of the season. And his shooting skills were pretty good too. When Sadio played the pass, Trent hit the ball first time, low and hard like an arrow into the bottom corner. *4–0!*

Goooooooooooooooooooaaaaaaaaaaaaaaaaallllllllllll lllllllllllll!!!!!!!!!!!!!!!!!!!

What a way to complete the victory! Trent jogged over to the Liverpool fans by the corner flag and celebrated in the style of one of the world's other football wonderkids, Kylian Mbappé. With a little jump, he planted his feet, folded his arms across his chest, and tried to look as cool as he could. That last part was hard, though, because Trent couldn't keep the smile off his face. He was on fire and Liverpool were getting closer and closer to the Premier League title!

Their lead at the top was now sixteen points. Surely, City couldn't catch them now? There was only one way to make sure, though – keep on winning:

1–0 vs Wolves,

2–0 vs Sheffield United,

1–0 vs Tottenham,

2–0 vs Manchester United…

Liverpool's lead was up to nineteen points! Surely, they could relax and start celebrating now? No, not yet. When West Ham went 2–1 up at Anfield, The Reds bounced straight back. They had the drive and determination to win every single match. That's what Champions were made of.

Robbo raced forward down the left and crossed to Mo. *2–2!*

Trent raced forward down the right and crossed to Sadio. *3–2!*

What wonderful teamwork! Although Liverpool's front three got a lot of the goals and a lot of the glory, they had incredible players in every position: Alisson in goal, Virgil at the back, Hendo, Gini, Naby and Fabinho in midfield, and, of course, the flying full backs, Robbo and Trent. Together, they formed the best side in the world.

'Come on, we're nearly there!' Klopp urged his team on. A few more wins and they would be crowned Champions of England for the first time in thirty years.

Even a surprise defeat to Watford couldn't dash Liverpool's title dreams. However, for a few months, it looked like COVID-19 might.

When the Premier League suddenly stopped in early March 2020 due to the coronavirus, Liverpool were twenty-two points clear and just days away from becoming Champions. What if they couldn't carry on? What if the season was over? Noooo, that would be so cruel!

For three long months, the Liverpool players stayed at home, training hard and hoping that they would get the chance to finish things off. In between his lockdown fitness sessions, Trent watched a lot of Netflix and played a lot of FIFA with Robbo and the others. That was fun, but it didn't even come close to the thrill of playing real football at Anfield. He couldn't wait for that.

At last, there was good news – it was safe for the Premier League to restart in June! But there was bad news too – there would be no supporters allowed in the stadiums. What, no fans?! What was the point of football without fans? It didn't feel right, but they had to carry on. Liverpool had a title to win and Trent was determined to give the people at home something to cheer about.

'Come on, let's do this!' he told himself as he walked out into an empty Goodison Park for a Merseyside Derby with a difference. Without the amazing atmosphere of a crowd, Liverpool could only draw 0–0 with their local rivals. Still, every single point was a step towards their target – the Premier League title.

'Closer,' Trent tweeted to the fans.

Three days later, Liverpool were back to their best in a 4–0 thrashing of Crystal Palace. Trent started it all in the first half by whipping another free kick into the top corner.

Goooooooooooooooooooaaaaaaaaaaaaaaaalllllllllllll llllllllllllll!!!!!!!!!!!!!!!!!!!!!!

It was so strange to celebrate without the familiar Anfield roar, but Trent still kissed the club badge on his shirt and leapt high into the air.

'Even closer,' he tweeted afterwards.

In fact, if City lost their next game against Chelsea, then the title would belong to Liverpool.

'I guess I'll have to be a Blue for one night only!' Trent joked as the players watched the game together in the garden of a local hotel.

'Yessssssss!' they cheered when Christian Pulisic scored.

'Nooooooo!' they groaned when Kevin De Bruyne equalised.

The match looked like it was heading for a disappointing 1–1 draw, until Abraham's shot was blocked on the line by Fernandinho's arm.

'Handball!' all of the Liverpool players screamed at the TV screen. 'That's a penalty!'

After checking with VAR, the referee pointed to the spot. Up stepped Willian to… SCORE – *2–1!*

At Stamford Bridge, the Chelsea players high-fived and bumped elbows, but that was nothing compared to the celebrations in the city of Liverpool. Their team had done it at last; they had won the Premier League title!

'Championssss!!!!' Trent tweeted the next morning with a funny video from the night before. Sleep could wait; he wanted to enjoy the moment and share it with the supporters. They had waited thirty long years for this.

Of all Trent's childhood dreams, winning the Premier League was definitely number one. As a boy, he had watched Liverpool come so close in 2009 and 2014, and he had then experienced that heartbreak for himself as a player in 2019. Well, one year later, that dream had just come true, just like all the others.

Trent had already achieved so much in his football career, and he was still only twenty-one years old. So, what would the future hold for the Premier League Young Player of the Year?

A World Cup victory with England? Hopefully!

More goals, assists and trophies for Liverpool? Definitely!

A move from right-back to his old central midfield role? Maybe!

But the most important thing for Trent was to keep playing for his beloved local team, and eventually, to become their leader, just like his hero, Stevie G. Until he could be appointed the proud captain of Liverpool Football Club, Trent would never quite be satisfied.

Liverpool

🏆 UEFA Champions League: 2018–19
🏆 UEFA Super Cup: 2019
🏆 FIFA Club World Cup: 2019
🏆 Premier League: 2019–20

Individual

🏆 Liverpool Young Player of the Season Award:
2016–17, 2017–18
🏆 PFA Premier League Team of the Year: 2018–19
🏆 UEFA Team of the Year: 2019

🏆 Premier League Young Player of the Season:
2019–20

🏆 Guinness World Record for the most assists by
a defender in a single season: 13 (2019–20)

ALEXANDER-ARNOLD

66   ## THE FACTS

NAME: Trent John Alexander-Arnold

DATE OF BIRTH: 07 October 1998

AGE: 22

PLACE OF BIRTH: West Derby, Liverpool

NATIONALITY: England

BEST FRIEND: Andrew 'Robbo' Robertson

CURRENT CLUB: Liverpool

POSITION: RB

THE STATS

Height (cm):	**180**
Club appearances:	**164**
Club goals:	**12**
Club trophies:	**4**
International appearances:	**12**
International goals:	**1**
International trophies:	**0**
Ballon d'Ors:	**0**

★ ★ ★ **HERO RATING: 87** ★ ★ ★

GREATEST MOMENTS

★ 1 15 AUGUST 2017, HOFFENHEIM 1–2 LIVERPOOL

Trent had already broken into the Liverpool first team, but this was the night when he showed that he was no ordinary right-back. In his first game of the new season, he stepped up and scored the free kick that led Liverpool to the Champions League Group Stage. A new hometown hero was born.

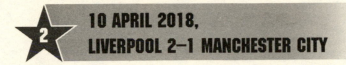

2 10 APRIL 2018, LIVERPOOL 2–1 MANCHESTER CITY

After a couple of poor performances against Marcus Rashford and Wilfried Zaha, Trent bounced back and proved that he could be a top defender in this Champions League quarter-final. In front of the home crowd at Anfield, he did a brilliant job against the speed and skill of Leroy Sané, and on this occasion won the battle.

3 27 FEBRUARY 2019, LIVERPOOL 5–0 WATFORD

Trent has certainly played in more competitive clashes than this, but this Premier League match meant a lot to him. Not only did he grab a hat-trick of amazing assists, but it was also the first time he heard the Anfield crowd sing his own special song: '*He's Alexander Arnooooold, The Scouser in our team!*'

4 7 MAY 2019, LIVERPOOL 4–0 BARCELONA

'The Miracle of Anfield' was an unforgettable night for everyone at Liverpool, but especially for Trent. He helped inspire the incredible comeback by setting up the second goal, and then he completed it with that quick-thinking corner to Divock Origi. Liverpool's local hero had led them back to the Champions League final again!

5 1 JUNE 2019, LIVERPOOL 2–0 TOTTENHAM

Back for his second Champions League final in two years, this was the night when Trent became a European Champion, just like his childhood hero, Steven Gerrard. Although he didn't score or set a goal up, Trent played his part at both ends of the pitch. At the final whistle, he sank to his knees – the lad from Liverpool's dream had just come true.

PLAY LIKE YOUR HEROES

TRENT ALEXANDER-ARNOLD'S
FREE KICK TECHNIQUE

STEP 1: First things first, you'll need to win a free kick in a good shooting position. If your attacking teammates aren't up to the job, then fly forward to win one yourself.

STEP 2: As soon as the referee blows the whistle, race over and grab the ball. This one's yours. And after you've scored a few beauties, no-one will argue anymore.

STEP 3: Place the ball down carefully and then start your routine: three steps backwards, pause, then one step to the right. You're in the zone now.

STEP 4: While you wait for the whistle, take a deep breath and look up at the target. In your head, imagine the ball flying into the corner of the net. Right, time to make it a reality…

STEP 5: Take short steps towards the ball and then swing that right leg back, ready to strike…

STEP 6: *BANG!* Put plenty of whip on your shot to send it up over the jumping wall and then down into the bottom corner.

STEP 7: *GOAL!* Kiss the badge on your shirt as you race over to celebrate with the fans. You're a local legend now!

TEST YOUR KNOWLEDGE

QUESTIONS

1. Other than football, what other game did Trent's dad teach him and his brothers?

2. Who did Liverpool play against when Trent made his first trip to Anfield, aged six, in 2005?

3. Name at least two positions that Trent played in before he became a right-back.

4. Which Liverpool legend coached Trent as a youngster and even wrote about him in his book?

5. Who was Liverpool's first choice of right-back before Trent?

6. Trent played his first full Premier League game against which of Liverpool's big rivals?

7. Name at least two other members of Liverpool's free-kick crew.

8. Which Manchester United forward gave Trent a game to forget in March 2018?

9. Trent played for England at the 2018 World Cup – true or false?

10. It was Trent's clever corner that led to Liverpool's winning goal in the 'Miracle of Anfield' against Barcelona, but who actually scored it?

11. How many team trophies did Trent win with Liverpool during the 2019–20 season?

Answers below. . . No cheating!

1. Chess 2. Juventus 3. Any of the following: central midfield, defensive midfield, centre-back, right wing and striker 4. Steven Gerrard 5. Nathaniel Clyne 6. Manchester United 7. Any of the following: Philippe Coutinho, Gini Wijnaldum, Alberto Moreno, Emre Can and Jordan Henderson. 8. Marcus Rashford 9. True – He made one appearance against Belgium in the group stage 10. Divock Origi 11. Three – the UEFA Super Cup, the FIFA Club World Cup and the Premier League